The Pennsylvania Germans

James Owen Knauss, Jr.'s Social History

Edited by

Don Heinrich Tolzmann

HERITAGE BOOKS
2014

HERITAGE BOOKS
AN IMPRINT OF HERITAGE BOOKS, INC.

Books, CDs, and more—Worldwide

For our listing of thousands of titles see our website
at
www.HeritageBooks.com

Published 2014 by
HERITAGE BOOKS, INC.
Publishing Division
5810 Ruatan Street
Berwyn Heights, Md. 20740

Copyright © 2001 Don Heinrich Tolzmann

All rights reserved. No part of this book may be reproduced or transmitted in any form or by any means, electronic or mechanical, including photocopying, recording or by any information storage and retrieval system without written permission from the author, except for the inclusion of brief quotations in a review.

International Standard Book Numbers
Paperbound: 978-0-7884-1706-1
Clothbound: 978-0-7884-6006-7

Contents

Editor's Introduction	v
Historical Introduction	xi
I. The Newspapers and Their Publishers	1
II. The Religion and the Religious Denominations of the Pennsylvania Germans	37
III. Charities and Humanitarian Organizations	58
IV. The Education and the Educational Facilities of the Pennsylvania Germans	73
V. Language	104
VI. Pennsylvania German Traits	119
VII. The Vocations of the Pennsylvania Germans	127
VIII. Political Ideals	141
Conclusion	168
Index	219

Editor's Introduction

This work represents a basic introduction to the Pennsylvania Germans in the 18th century as reflected in the German-American press. It has long since been considered an essential source on the topic, but was somewhat inaccessible as it appeared in the publications of the Pennsylvania German Society, which have long since been out of print.[1] Also, it's use was limited by the fact that it was not indexed. The purpose of this work is to provide access to this important work, and also to enhance its use by means of an index.

This is basically a two-tier history: On one level it provides a descriptive analysis of the German-American press of Pennsylvania, and on another it provides an in depth analysis of who the readers of this press were. On the first, the history and the characteristics of the newspapers and their publishers are described, thereby providing an invaluable and in-depth history of the Pennsylvania German press.

On the second, the religious life, charities and humanitarian organizations, edcuation, the language, occupational distribution, and political life of the Pennsylania Germans are explored. In addition, a checklist of 18th century German-American newspapers in Pennsylvania and neighboring states is provided, as well as the U.S. libraries holding them. This along makes this source an essential guide to the history of the Pennsylania Germans in general, especially with the checklist of colonial German-American newspaper.

As this work covers the German-American press and all aspects of Pennsylvania German life, the reader finds reference to the names of the leading figures in colonial German-American life, all of whom are accessed by means of the index.

Due to the fact that half of the colonial German element resided in Pennsylvania, this work takes on greater importance as it is central to understanding the history of the colonial German-American experience in general.[2]

Today, approximately 40% of the population of the state of Pennsylvania claims German heritage, thereby making the German element the largest ethnic component in the state. The Pennsylvania Germans, therefore, are not only of historical interest, but continue to play an important role to the present time, and their foundations are found in the 18th century.

The Pennsylvania Germans also occupy an important place in the annals of German-American history for many reasons, but primarily as a result of the fact that Pennsylvania became the focal point of German immigration and settlement in the colonial era. Indeed, approximately one-half of the colonial German element resided there. At the time of the American Revolution, the Pennsylvania Germans constituted a full one-third of the population of Pennsylvania.[3]

The Pennsylvania Germans, hence, came to be the defining group in the foundational period of the German-American experience. Another important aspectd about the Pennsylvania Germans is how they have so successfully acclimated to America, and at the same time preserved their German heritage and identity.[4]

Although Germans first came to America and landed at Jamestown, Virginia in 1608, and then later settled at New Netherlands, New Sweden, and elsewhere, it was in Pennsylvania on the 6th of October 1683 that the first permanent all-German settlement was established in America at Germantown, now part of Philadelphia.[5]

Thereafter, Germantown became the major German-American social, cultural, and political center, and it would remain so into the 19th century, and even later would still be an important German-American center. The Pennsylvania Germans have always been a fascinating topic to the general public, as well as to historians. In completing my *German-Americana: A Bibliorapky*, I noted that in terms of state histories dealing with German-Americans, more than 21% deal with the Pennsylvania Germans.[6]

It has been my goal to make a wide variety of works dealing with German-American history available and accessible once again, especially as a result of the increased interest in the German heritage. In so doing, the editor has selected a number of classics in the field of German-American history, and this work is an excellent edition to this series of works.

Notes

1. This work was first published as: James Owen Knauss, Mr., *Social Conditions Among the Pennsylvania germans in the Eighteenth Century as Revealed in the German Newspapers Published in America.* The Pennsylvania German Society Proceedings, Vol. 29. (Lancaster, Pa.: The Pennsylvania German Society, 1922).

2. For a general German-American history, see Don Heinrich Tolzmann, *The German-American Experience.* (Amherst, New York: Humanity Books, 2000).

3. For a survey of their role in the American revolution, see Don Heinrich Tolzmann, ed., *The German-American Soldier in the Wars of the U.S.: J.G. Rosengarten's History.* (Bowie, MD: Heritage Books, Inc., 1996).

4. For references to works on the Pennsylvania Germans, see Michael Keresztesi and Gary R. Cocozzoli, *German-American History and Life. A Guide to Information Sources.* (Detroit: Gale Research Co., 1980).

5. These early settlements are discussed in greater detail in Tolzmann, *German-American Experience*, pp. 31-79.

6. See my *German-Americana: A Bibliography.* (Metuchen, NJ: Scarecrow Press, 1975).

ABBREVIATIONS.

A   = *Der Unpartheyische Reading Adler* (1796–1800).
AS   = *Der Americanische Staatsbothe* (1800).
Ba   = Bailey's *Das Pennsylvanische Zeitungsblat* (1778).
CW = *Die Chesnuthiller Wochenschrift* (1790–1794).
DP   = *Der Deutsche Porcupein* (1798–1799).
GP   = *Der General Post-Bothe* (1790).
GZ   = *Die Germantauner Zeitung* (1785–1790).
GZ_2 = *Die Germantauner Zeitung* (1790–1793).
H   = Hütter's *Der Lancaster Correspondent* (1799–1800).
M   = Miller's *Staatsbote* (1762–1779).
NUL = *Neue Unpartheyische Lancäster Zeitung* (1787–1797).
NUR = *Neue Unpartheyische Readinger Zeitung* (1789–1800).
PC   = *Philadelphische Correspondenz* (1781–1790).
PC_2 = *Philadelphische Correspondenz* (1790–1797).
PC_3 = *Philadelphische Correspondenz* (1798–1800).
PC_4 = *Philadelphische Correspondenz* (1800).
PS   = *Philadelphisches Staatsregister* (1779–1780).
PZ   = *Philadelphische Zeitung* (1755–1757).
S   = Saur's paper (1739–1777).
UH = *Die Unpartheyische Härrisburg Zeitung* (1799–1800).

PREFACE.

TWO considerations have rendered this subject especially attractive to me. In the first place, none of the historians of the Germans in America has given it the attention which it deserved. Kuhns in his "German and Swiss Settlements of Colonial Pennsylvania" devotes one page to the subject of newspapers and mentions only one by name, Saur's colonial paper. Faust in his "German Element in the United States" discusses the German newspapers of the eighteenth century somewhat more in detail, although he does not mention half of them. In fact, it was Professor Faust himself who suggested the topic to me, because he knew what an imperfect knowledge historians possessed of this subject. Needless to say, neither Professor Faust nor Professor Kuhns derived the material for their accurate works from the periodical publications. Professor Oswald Seidensticker, the pioneer historian of the period, obtained much of his material from the old

Pennsylvania German papers, but he drew almost all of it from Saur's and Miller's colonial papers, and did not by any means exhaust even these papers as a source of historical information. As to bibliographies of these newspapers, there are only two that deserve serious consideration. Seidensticker in his "First Century of German Printing in America" names about five sixths of the periodical publications, although his usual reliability is not apparent in his statements concerning the papers published in the last two decades of the century. Moreover, he often does not tell us where the files are located and never describes the state of their completeness. The second bibliography was compiled by Daniel Miller about twenty-five years after the appearance of Seidensticker's work in *Der deutsche Pionier*. He usually followed his predecessor very closely, often making the same mistakes, even minor ones such as a wrong initial or a wrong date.

The second reason for my interest in the subject is a purely personal one. As a descendant of one of these early German immigrants, Ludwig Knauss, who arrived in this country as early as 1723, I have always felt a keen personal interest in that extraordinary group of Americans, the so-called Pennsylvania "Dutch." Reared in a rural community where the patois is still extensively spoken, I know their weakness and their strength. I have always felt the injustice done to them by those who have not been able to penetrate behind their stolid reserve. As an example of this injustice, we may well take the novels of Helen Reimensnyder Martin. I make no objection to her works as fiction and, as such, I have read several with much pleasure; but when she leads people to believe that her novels give an accurate picture of the ordinary

Pennsylvania-German community, it seems to me time to disagree. Desiring to investigate first-hand records concerning the ancestors of these people, who are American to the core, I gladly availed myself of a source of information which has thus far scarcely been discovered.

In writing down the results of my investigations, I have tried to be fair in giving an account of both the good and the bad qualities of the Pennsylvania Germans. Newspapers present pitfalls as well as advantages in the search for truth. There is great danger for the historian if he does not strive for an unbiased viewpoint. He must not expect to gain an accurate idea of the social conditions in a community exclusively from newspapers, since the demand for reports of unusual events, or, in other words, for news, causes the papers to give us a much distorted view of existing conditions.

My thanks are due to the librarians of the various libraries mentioned in my newspaper bibliography for the courteous treatment they accorded to me in my researches, and especially to the following library officers, whom I may have tried sorely with my unrelenting correspondence: Mr. Clarence S. Brigham, of the American Antiquarian Society, Worcester, Massachusetts; Mr. Ernest Spofford, of the Historical Society of Pennsylvania, Philadelphia; Mr. Thomas Lynch Montgomery, of the State Library, Harrisburg, Pennsylvania; Dr. I. M. Hays, of the American Philosophical Society, Philadelphia; Mr. Andrew Shaaber, of the Berks County Historical Society, Reading, Pennsylvania; Miss Lottie Bausman, of the Lancaster County Historical Society, Lancaster, Pennsylvania, and Miss Lina Hertzog, of the Deutsche Gesellschaft, Philadelphia. I want to give my thanks to Dr. Albert Cook

Myers, of Moylan, Pennsylvania, for especially valuable suggestions concerning repositories of German American newspapers of the eighteenth century; to Mr. M. A. Gruber, of Washington, D. C.; Mr. Ethan Allen Weaver, of Germantown, Pennsylvania; Reverend Dr. William J. Hinke, of Auburn, New York, and Mr. A. K. Hostetter, of Lancaster, Pennsylvania, for giving me important information about some of the early newspapers and their editors, and to Dr. George C. Keidel, of Washington, D. C., for helpful suggestions about the arrangement of various parts of the monograph. I owe a special debt of gratitude to Dr. Albert Bernhardt Faust, of Cornell University, who, as mentioned above, first suggested this subject to me, for his inspiring guidance and sympathetic criticism. Prof. Carl Becker, of Cornell University, gave me the benefit of his searching and constructive criticism. Prof. Paul R. Pope, of Cornell, carefully reviewed the manuscript and gave me many valuable criticisms while I was revising the first draft. Finally, I want to thank the many friends, unnamed but unforgettable, who have kindly answered my letters of inquiry.

JAMES O. KNAUSS.

CORNELL UNIVERSITY,
February 22, 1918.

CHAPTER I.

THE NEWSPAPERS AND THEIR PUBLISHERS.

THE German Americans of the eighteenth century, whose descendants of the present day are generally known as Pennsylvania Germans, published a creditable number of newspapers. It has been definitely established that a total of thirty-eight[1] German newspapers existed at various times between 1732 and the end of the century. Indeed, it is probable that even more were published, since some of the less important ones, which were in existence for only a very brief period, may have vanished without leaving any traces.

I have been able to locate copies and reprints of twenty-five of the eighteenth century German American papers, but only very few copies of many of these twenty-five papers have been preserved. In fact, most of the material for this monograph has been drawn from six leading journals, of which, fortunately, many issues are on file in various libraries. The two of these that were published before the Revolutionary War were Saur's paper, of which about three hundred and fifty issues between 1739 and 1777 are extant, and Miller's *Staatsbote*, of which about nine hundred issues between 1762 and 1779 have been

---

[1] There were thirty-nine papers, if we consider the thrice-a-week edition of a paper as distinct from the weekly edition.

located. The other four important papers were the *Philadelphische Correspondenz* (more than nine hundred and fifty issues are in existence that were published between 1781 and 1800), the *Germantauner Zeitung* (two hundred and forty-six issues between 1785 and 1793 are extant), the *Neue Unpartheyische Lancäster Zeitung*, including the continuation of the paper under different titles (about four hundred and sixty-five issues between 1787 and 1800 have survived), and the *Neue Unpartheyische Readinger Zeitung* (about six hundred issues between 1789 and 1800 are in existence). To this group of post-bellum papers may be added the *Reading Adler*, which, however, is not very important for the eighteenth century, since its publication was begun only four years before the end of the century. Of the remaining eighteen newspapers, none were in existence more than six years and some less than a year. Of ten of these, I have found five or less copies, and of none of the remaining eight more than one hundred and ten. However, it is usually easy to form a fairly accurate estimate of their characteristics, even if only a few copies have been preserved.

Most of the publishers were men with a high sense of responsibility. Their aim usually was to improve the social, political, intellectual, moral and religious conditions of their German American countrymen. For instance, in the first number of Franklin's *Philadelphische Zeitung* (May 6, 1732), L. Timothee, the editor, advises his subscribers to preserve the copies of the paper and to have them bound at the end of the year, since he intends to print in them an account of the founding of the province and a résumé of all privileges, rights and laws of the colony. This information, in addition to the chronicle of contemporary events, the editor declares, will aid the readers in obtaining a more intelligent comprehension of the events of the following years. Thus the earliest German American newspaper which has been located was published for the purpose of making the Germans better citizens of the province of Pennsylvania.

Franklin's *Zeitung* did not thrive, probably because the time was not yet ripe for a successful German paper. A contributing cause of its failure was perhaps its German, fearfully and wonderfully made. As an example of this, the first sentence of the only advertisement in the second issue will suffice, "Es wird hiemit bekandt gemacht, dasz Hendrick Van Bebber, welcher viele Jahre her als Doctor Medicinae mit gutem success practicieret, hat sich hier zur wohn niedergesetzet." Louis Thimothee, the editor, was a protege of Franklin, who also made him librarian of the new Philadelphia Library, and later, after the death of Thomas Whitemarsh, sent him to South Carolina to take charge of his printing office in Charleston.[2]

In 1739 Christoph Saur started in Germantown, Pennsylvania, the first German American newspaper which lived beyond the experimental stage. His *Der Hoch-Deutsch Pennsylvanische Geschicht-Schreiber, Oder: Sammlung Wichtiger Nachrichten aus dem Natur- und Kirchen- Reich* was in existence from 1739 to 1777. It was published by its founder up to the time of his death, on September 25, 1758, after which it was continued by his son, Christoph. The older Saur, according to the obituary notice[3] by his

[2] See Julius F. Sachse's article, "The First German Newspaper Published in America" (PROCEEDINGS OF PENNSYLVANIA GERMAN SOCIETY, Vol. X, p. 44).

[3] S 9–30–58. (For list of abbreviations used in referring to newspapers, see my newspaper bibliography and page vii. Whenever possible I give the number of the issue, not the date of the issue.)

son, was sixty-four years old when he died. He had spent the last thirty-four years of his life in Pennsylvania. The son paid a glowing tribute to his father's conscientiousness and promised to attempt to continue his policy. The second Christoph Saur conducted the business up to the first years of the Revolutionary War, when he was succeeded by his two sons, Christoph Saur, Jr. (the third), and Peter Saur. The exact date on which the transfer to the sons was made can not be determined, because no copies of the paper have been located between the issue of September 11, 1776, and that of February 26, 1777, the former of which still bore the name of Christoph Saur, while the latter was published by the sons.

The Saur paper was undoubtedly the most influential German journal of the period. As a source of historical information, it is probably also the most valuable German paper of the century, because the older Saur, far from being a slavish imitator of other publishers, printed what he thought was in keeping with the ideals which he expressed in the first number dated August 20, 1739. In his address to the readers he assures them that he does not intend to publish the paper as a sacrifice to the idols of curiosity and of a desire to hear, see, know and say something new, nor will he publish it for the selfish purpose of attaining fame. He intends to publish the most useful and the most important stories and occurrences, so that they may create deeper impression and more meditation.

This moral purpose was a distinguishing characteristic of the paper during the whole forty years of its existence. For instance, in Number 106 (March 16, 1749), Saur says he will not print confessions of counterfeiters because this would teach other rascals how to make spurious money.

The tendency of the paper to moralize was so pronounced that its opponents attacked the second Saur for this reason. They claimed[4] that he refused to publish news to which he could not attach a suitable moral.

The Saurs were Dunkers or German Baptists. Faithful to the doctrines of this sect, the Saur paper always advocated non-resistance, attacked higher education and a specially educated clergy, but ever actively supported charitable organizations and such movements which the publishers believed would promote the physical and moral welfare of the community.[5] They were scrupulously honest. The older Saur changed the title of the paper from *Geschicht-Schreiber* (Chronicler) to *Berichte* (News), because it was impossible to prevent inaccurate news from getting into the paper.[6] Between April 9, 1762, and August 1, 1766, the second Christoph Saur changed the word "Wichtiger" (important) in the title to "Wahrscheinlicher" (probable), doubtless because he thought the former adjective was not sufficiently accurate.

That Saur's paper was very influential can readily be believed when we remember that the German Dunkers and Mennonites[7] were in those early days very strong in numbers and influence. In 1753 the paper had four thousand readers.[8] Saur's opponents also admit the strength of the paper's influence over the people. Heinrich Melchior Mühlenberg, in a letter written in 1754 to Benjamin Franklin, deplores the influence which Saur was wielding even over the Lutherans and the Reformed by means of

---

[4] M 294, 296.
[5] See Chapters II, III and IV.
[6] S 66.
[7] The Mennonites were closely allied with the Dunkers in doctrine. See Chapter II.
[8] S 11-1-53.

his newspaper. He declares that despite all efforts to undermine this influence, Saur still retains the advantage, turning the Germans against their clergy and against everybody who endeavors to reduce them to order in church and state affairs.[9]

Prompted by his intensely religious nature, the second Saur commenced in 1764 the publication of a religious magazine, which was probably the first of its kind in America. In the "Vorrede" to *Ein Geistliches Magazien* he announces his intention of publishing it whenever time and circumstances will permit, asks his readers to write articles for it, and promises to distribute the copies gratuitously so that he may gain no temporal profit thereby.

While the second Saur was a non-resistant, like all orthodox Dunkers, we have no adequate proof that he opposed the War of Independence, since only five issues of the paper for the years 1775, 1776 and 1777 have been located. It is probable that he preserved strict neutrality, not supporting either of the belligerents, but simply publishing the news as he received it. We can well imagine that such a course was very unsatisfactory to the patriots, who began to regard him as an enemy. Hence his influence, which had been declining for the preceding ten years, disappeared almost entirely. He became a marked man, when his sons, Christoph Saur, the third, and Peter Saur, published the old paper under a new name, *Der Pennsylvanische Staats-Courier*, and made it a most rabid and coarse Tory paper during the British occupation of Philadelphia. We are inclined to wonder what caused this change in attitude on the part of the sons. Was it due to an overwhelming conviction of the justice of the British point of

[9] See H. W. Smith's "Life and Correspondence of the Rev. William Smith, D.D." Vol. I. p. 66.

view, or to anger at the taunts and insults flung at them by hot-headed patriots during the first two years of the struggle? So far as the father is concerned, it is generally believed that he remained completely neutral during these stormy times. Certainly his actions were those of an innocent man. On May 23, 1778, twenty-four days before the British left Philadelphia, he returned to his home in Germantown within the American lines[10]—an act of folly for any man who was not completely unconscious of any guilt. On the British evacuation of Philadelphia the Americans confiscated the property of the father and his sons. When Henrich Miller, the publisher of the *Staatsbote*, returned to the city he attempted to secure the press of Christoph Saur, the third.[11] The goods of the second Saur were sold by the authorities at public sale, beginning on Monday, August 24, 1778. They consisted, among other things, of feather-beds, bedclothes, chairs, tables, writing tables, buffets, kitchen utensils, a printing press, Bibles and all his publications.[12] Thus ended the influence of the Saurs, the most remarkable family of German printers in the colonial period. Christoph Saur, the second, died on August 26, 1784, poor but faithful to the tenets of his sect.

In the fall of 1790 Samuel Saur,[13] the youngest son of the second Saur, attempted to resurrect the prestige of the Saur family by starting *Die Chesnuthiller Wochenschrift*, which followed the same general principles as the Germantown paper. It contained much religious material, pub-

---

[10] McCulloch's Additional Memoranda, p. 136.

[11] See broadside of July 22, 1778 by Henrich Miller, in possession of P. H. S.

[12] M 880.

[13] He was born in Germantown on March 30, 1767, and died in Baltimore, October 12, 1820.

lished articles in favor of non-resistance and bitterly attacked higher education. It is quite probable that his *Philadelphier Wochenblat* and his Baltimore paper had the same characteristics.

All pre-revolutionary German newspapers may be divided into two groups, the Saur papers and those of his opponents. The latter, of which, unfortunately, but few copies published prior to 1762 are in existence, favored higher education and upheld a policy of military defense. They were the organs of the Lutherans, the Reformed and the Moravians.

Benjamin Franklin was often the financial backer of these papers. Whether this is true of *Das Hoch-deutsche Pennsylvanische Journal* (1743) and of Gotthart Armbrüster's weekly of 1748, I have found no means of ascertaining. Franklin probably had an interest in Johann Böhm's *Philadelphier Teutsche Fama*, for Franklin and Böhm were associated in a publishing company at that time.[14] His name appeared as publisher of the Philadelphia bi-lingual paper of 1751 and of the *Philadelphische Zeitung* (1755–1757). It has been definitely proved that he was also the controlling factor in Müller and Holland's *Die Lancastersche Zeitung* of 1752–1753.[15] Copies of only the last two papers have been located. In these we look in vain for a strong personality, such as belonged to Saur. They generally give the news as colorlessly as possible. The *Philadelphische Zeitung* printed detailed accounts of the doings of the provincial assembly and the progress of the French and Indian War. There seems to be no reliable information about the publishers of *Die Lancastersche Zeitung*. We know absolutely nothing about

[14] Adv. in S 107.
[15] Sachse's "The German Sectarians," Vol. II, p. 443 ff.

S. Holland. H. Müller, who was at first associated with Holland, was probably Henrich Miller, who later became famous as the publisher of the *Staatsbote*.[16] Anthon Armbrüster, who published the *Philadelphische Zeitung* in partnership with Franklin, was a brother of Gotthart Armbrüster. Anthon continued in the printing business up to 1767 or 1768. In 1762 he was publishing *Die Pennsylvanische Fama*.[17] He died in 1796. The Reverend John F. Handschuh was the editor of the *Philadelphische Zeitung*. He was a Lutheran minister, who had had charges in Lancaster and Germantown. In 1755 he was made professor of French at the academy which later became the University of Pennsylvania. From 1758 to his death in 1764 he was pastor of St. Michael's Lutheran Church in Philadelphia.[18]

When Henrich Miller published the first number of *Der Wöchentliche Philadelphische Staatsbote*, on January 18, 1762, the Saur newspaper at last faced a dangerous competitor. Miller was peculiarly qualified to be the most influential German printer and publisher of the stormy days preceding the Revolution. He had a thorough knowledge of the mechanical part of printing, having spent many years in the printing business at various places in Europe and America.[19] As early as 1715, when only thirteen years of age, he left his native Waldeck and entered upon his apprenticeship at Basel, Switzerland. When he departed from Basel for Zurich in 1721, he became a wanderer for thirty-nine years. In the fall of

[16] See below.
[17] M 34, 35.
[18] M 144.
[19] The materials for the following biographical sketch were found in Miller's advertisement in S 6-19-61, in his farewell to his readers in M 920 and in the obituary notice in PC 51.

1721 he went to Leipzig, in 1722 to Altona, in 1725 to London, in 1729 to Altona again, in 1732 to Switzerland, where he worked at his trade in Basel, Geneva and Zurich. In 1738 we find him in Hamburg, in 1739 in Amsterdam, from which place he proceeded to Paris by way of Antwerp and Brussels. In November, 1740, he arrived at London via Calais and Dover. Then he embarked for America, where on his arrival he began to work for Franklin. In 1742 he returned to Germany again. From 1747 to 1751 he worked at his trade in England, Scotland and Ireland. In 1751 he came to Philadelphia again. There is a conflict of authorities regarding Miller's activities during his second stay in America. His advertisement states that he worked for Hall and Bradfort (sic) in Philadelphia and for Saur in Germantown. His obituary notice, however, records that he started a printing establishment. In 1754 he returned to Germany for the last time. In 1756 he operated his own printing press in England, where he published a semi-weekly German newspaper for fourteen thousand Hanoverian and Hessian troops who were quartered in that country during the whole summer. On September 12, 1760, he came to Philadelphia a third time and started a printing establishment of his own.

These long years spent as a journeyman not only made him thoroughly acquainted with his trade, but broadened his views immensely. In this respect he was far the superior of the younger Saur, who had had no such opportunities to widen his horizon, having lived all his life among the sectarians in provincial Pennsylvania. In addition to Miller's experience and broad-mindedness, he was presumably a shrewd business man. Starting with hardly any surplus money,[20] he succeeded in becoming the most influ-

[20] M 65.

ential German colonial printer. From the first he tried to introduce his paper throughout the English colonies. He had agents at various places in Pennsylvania, New Jersey, New York, Maryland, Virginia, South Carolina, Georgia and Nova Scotia.[21]

There was at least one more reason why Miller's paper was successful. The later German immigrants had been largely Lutheran, Reformed and Moravian. After having spent ten, twenty or thirty years in the country, these people had attained a certain degree of affluence, so that even their proverbial economy allowed them to buy newspapers. They naturally chose to read a good newspaper published by a non-sectarian rather than one published by such an uncompromising sectarian as Saur.

The most striking feature of the *Staatsbote* is the fact that it contains very little news that gives us an insight into the life and customs of the contemporary German Americans as distinguished from their English neighbors. Perhaps this is due to the circumstance that Miller had spent only very few years in the colony. To a certain degree he had become a cosmopolitan through his long wanderings, so that as an editor he was not interested in the every-day life of the people whom he served. We must not conclude, however, that Miller was not interested in the welfare of the Germans. For instance, his paper mentioned with favor the organization of a *Deutsche Gesellschaft*, which had as its chief aim the amelioration of conditions among the German immigrants.[22]

According to Miller's greetings to the readers in the first number of the *Staatsbote*, he wanted by his trade to serve God and his neighbors (especially the Germans liv-

[21] M 1 ff.
[22] M 153, 155, 157 et al.

ing in this part of the world, so far removed from their fatherland) with fidelity and to the best of his ability. He maintained that a Christian could promote by means of a newspaper not only the general welfare, but also the glory of God. He promised to make the news in his paper as accurate as possible and occasionally to extol the virtues of a Christian and of a citizen. This proclaimed religious aim would lead us to expect editorial notes, moralizing on various events, similar to those found in Saur's paper. Instead of moral reflections, however, Miller inserted in his paper paragraphs describing the location and appearance of places mentioned in the foreign dispatches. Sometimes he also appended observations on great political events of Europe.

There is no question that Miller's chief interest lay in making his German countrymen intelligent citizens of the province. He desired to make them acquainted with political conditions. He printed unusually full reports of the doings of the Pennsylvania Provincial Assembly, occasionally issuing supplements for this purpose.[23] During the stirring times between 1765 and 1779 he was always on the side of liberty.[24] He was continually calling the attention of the Germans to the fact that they lived in a good country. "What great cause we have to thank God for His kindness and for the good land which He has given to us."[25]

Since Miller was politically inclined, we may safely assume that he copied much from the English papers of the period. This belief is strengthened by a notice in the *Staatsbote* of October 15, 1771, that the issue of the pre-

[23] M 118, 120 for example.
[24] See Chapter VIII.
[25] M 516.

ceding week had contained a misstatement owing to the fact that the publisher had copied the item from the English papers.

The War for Independence brought with it hard times for Miller, as it did for so many others. One of his chief difficulties was the scarcity of labor. On December 3, 1776, he warned his subscribers that he might have to discontinue the regular weekly issue, because he could not find any helper. On April 21, 1779, he uttered a similar complaint. The increased pressure of hard times was also indicated by the change in the price of the newspaper from six shillings to eight shillings[26] and later to two pounds five shillings.[27]

When the British threatened Philadelphia, Miller fled on September 25, 1777, leaving all his possessions[28] behind him. Returning on July 4, 1778, he found himself robbed of his presses and of most of his books. He says a certain James Robertson took the better press, while the robbers, Christoph Saur, Jr., & Co., seized much of the remaining one. However, this did not deter him from beginning the publication of the paper again on August 5, 1778. In this number he greets his friends thus:

Werthe Freunde, Nachdem ich mich einigermassen von der Bestürzung in welche mich der Raub meiner Druckerey gesetzt hat, erholt habe, will ich getrost, in Gottes Namen wieder anfangen, ihnen nach Vermögen, mit meinen übrig gelassenen Buchstaben und einer geborgten Presse zu dienen.

The paper was published regularly up to May 26, 1779, when it suspended publication. As early as April 28 he printed this notice:

[26] M 875.
[27] M 886.
[28] See broadside by Miller dated July 22, 1778.

Noth hat kein Geboth. Wenn meine resp. Kunden die Zeitung nicht richtig krigen oder ich sie aufgeben musz, mögen sie vest glauben, dasz meine schlechten Umstände, mein hohes Alter, Leibesschwäche, und dasz ich ohne Hülfe bin, es verursachen.

Miller probably left Philadelphia in the fall of 1779, for he insisted that all his creditors should call for their money before the end of August, 1779.[29] He died at Bethlehem on Sunday, March 31, 1782, as his obituary notice[30] says, "ein um das Publicum und besonders die Deutschen sehr wohl verdienter Mann."

His farewell[31] to the readers of his paper deserves to be quoted in full, because it shows the spirit which animated the man.

Allerseits Hochgeehrte Herren, Freunde und Landsleute.

Sie wissen dasz der Sabbath so alt ist als die Schöpfung. Es heiszt von dem Herrn unserm Gott selbst: Er ruhete am siebenten Tage von allen seinen Werken die Er machte. Die Felder hatten ihren Sabbath; die Thiere genossen ihn; er ist ganz besonders um des Menschen willen eingesetzt; und wird mit der Zeit die Sehnsucht aller geschaffenen Wesen. Nur der Hüter Israel schläfet und schlummert nicht.

Wenn heutiges tags ein Mann sein 60stes Jahr zurückgelegt hat, so hält man dafür sein Sabbath solte angehen, und er selbst nicht mehr arbeiten, sondern nur zusehen dasz andere für ihn ihre Arbeit recht machen.

Ich bin nun, werthe Freunde, nicht weit von 80 Jahren, beynahe durch den Raub meiner Druckerey in meinem Beruf ruinirt, ohne gehörige Hülfe und Unterstützung: Was deucht Ihnen? Sie werden mirs gewisz nicht verdenken dasz ich mich nach meiner Sabbaths-ruhe sehne, und zu dem End ich es nöthig erachte die Zeitung aufzugeben, als eine Arbeit die pünktlich an einem bestimmten Tag fertig seyn musz.

[29] M 920.
[30] PC 51.
[31] M 920.

Die Abfertigung eines Staatsboten gehört für einen frischen, hurtigen Mann. So lang ich ein solcher war, geehrte Landsleute, diente ich Ihnen herzlich gern; hab auch wirklich bey 50 Jahr fast immer mit Zeitungen zu thun gehabt, ehedem in der Schweiz und Deutschland; und als in dem letztern Kriege zwischen Frankreich und England einmal 14000 Man Hanöverischer und Heszischer Truppen den Sommer hindurch in England lagen, bediente ich, auf Ersuchen des Stabes, ihre beyden Lager zweymal in der Woche mit einer Deutschen Zeitung.

Die Leute mögen Zeitungen ansehen wie sie wollen, ich habe sie immer für gemein nützlich gehalten, und die Aufsetzung und Ausgabe derselben für eine angenehme Beschäftigung eines Mannes von einem mittelmäszigen Alter.

Hat meine geringe Zeitungsarbeit, geehrte und werthe Landsleute, Ihren Beyfall gehabt, wird es mir ein besonder Vergnügen seyn; ganz das Gegentheil vermuth ich nicht, sondern glaube es ist doch manchen damit gedient gewesen.

Ich habe gethan was ich konte, danke meinen Freunden und Gönnern für Ihre Ermunterung, und bitte mir Ihre fernere Gewogenheit aus bey eräugnender Gelegenheit.

Meine Treue zu diesem Lande ist, wie ich hoffe, genugsam bekannt; und was meine Achtung für die Deutsche Nation betrifft, so möcht ich wünschen ein jeder Deutsche verstünde ihre Würdigkeit. Ich meines theils verharre dieses ganzen Landes doch vorzüglich der Deutschen, treuergebener Freund und Diener.

H. MILLER.

Besides *Der Pennsylvanische Staats Courier,* mentioned above, three other German papers were published at various times during the War for Independence—*Das Pennsylvanische Zeitungs-Blat, Die Pennsylvanische Gazette* and *Philadelphisches Staatsregister.* None of them continued to the end of the war.

Das Pennsylvanische Zeitungs-Blat was published in Lancaster during the first half of 1778, while the British were in possession of Philadelphia. It contained war news almost exclusively. The publisher notified the public that he would stop publishing the paper on June 24, 1778, because there had not been enough demand for it since the enemy had evacuated Philadelphia.[32] Francis Bailey, the publisher, learned the trade at Ephrata, Lancaster County, Pennsylvania.[33] In the eighties he published an English paper, *Freeman's Journal*, in Philadelphia.

Die Pennsylvanische Gazette made its first appearance on February 3, 1779. The publisher, John Dunlap, probably intended to issue it as the successor to the defunct Saur paper, since he also continued the editions of the Saur almanac under the old title. I do not know whether more than one issue was ever published, but it was no longer in existence in July of that year. The first number, the only one I have located, is full of war news, and the advertisements are limited almost entirely to the offering of rewards for the apprehension of thieves and other criminals.

The *Philadelphisches Staatsregister*, published by Melchior Steiner and Charles Cist, had an existence of almost a year and perhaps of almost two years. In form and content it does not differ essentially from the two last-mentioned papers. In the first number, dated July 21, 1779, the publishers say that since there is not a single German paper in America at the present time, they will publish one even in these hard times for a quarter of a year in order to find out whether they will receive sufficient support to continue it. The same firm had intended[34] to start a German paper in 1776, but apparently never had secured the five hundred subscribers necessary to carry out the project.

[32] Ba 21.
[33] McCulloch's Additional Memoranda.
[34] S 645 and M 781.

The firm was dissolved in 1781, after having been in existence since December, 1775.[35] Cist[36] was born in St. Petersburg in 1738. When he came to America he joined the Moravians. After 1781 he continued in the printing business on his own account. In 1784, with others, he published an English monthly, the *American Herald;* in 1786, another one, *Columbian Magazine*. In the administration of Adams he was appointed the printer for the national government. He died in 1805 and was buried at Bethlehem. Melchior Steiner was the son of the Reverend Conrad Steiner, former pastor of the Reformed Church of Philadelphia.[37] William McCulloch says both father and son were born in Switzerland.[38] After the dissolution of the firm, Steiner and Cist, Melchior Steiner commenced the publication of the *Gemeinnützige Philadelphische Correspondenz*. In 1797 or 1798 he severed connection with this firm and, according to Seidensticker, went to Washington, where he died in 1807.[39]

With the year 1781 a new period in the history of German American newspapers began. They became increasingly political in nature as the end of the century approached. As a rule, we look in vain for the originality which is found in the older Saur's paper and even in Miller's *Staatsbote*. The number of newspapers increased from one in 1781 to at least thirteen at the beginning of 1800. Before 1781 all the German newspapers had been published in Germantown and Philadelphia, with two or

---

[35] See advertisement in M 758.

[36] The material for this biographical sketch is taken from "Geschichte der deutschen Gesellschaft," pp. 469–470.

[37] See Chapter II.

[38] McCulloch's Additional Memoranda, p. 240.

[39] Seidensticker's "First Century of German Printing in America." p. 96.

three exceptions. At the beginning of 1800 we find them also appearing in Baltimore, Hagerstown, Hanover, York, Lancaster, Harrisburg, Reading and Easton.

The paper that ushered in the new period was the *Gemeinnützige Philadelphische Correspondenz*, which probably made its initial appearance on May 2, 1781. It was destined to have an existence of more than thirty-one years. Melchior Steiner, the publisher, was fortunate in securing the Lutheran ministers, the Reverends Kunze and Helmuth, as editors of his paper, either at the time that he issued the first number or shortly thereafter. They retained the editorship for several years.[40] It was probably due to their able supervision that the publication became noted for its efficient news service. In the fall of 1782 it could boast that English papers were printing translations of its news. The various items actually appeared earlier in the German paper than in its English contemporaries. This is in marked contrast with the earlier German papers, in which the news appeared about two weeks later than in the English papers.[41] The *Philadelphische Correspondenz* became so influential that by 1788 it had a considerable number of readers in Germany.[42]

Gradually, however, the standard of the paper declined, so that Steiner announced[43] a change of editors in 1790. When the new editor, C. C. Reiche,[44] took charge in October of that year, the paper became a semi-weekly. Steiner promised that it would be conducted on an entirely new plan, that the editor would explain and comment upon the

[40] "Hallesche Nachrichten;" Vol. II, p. 786.
[41] PC 82.
[42] PC 380.
[43] PC 486.
[44] See below.

various news items. These explanations stopped almost entirely with the issue of November 5, 1790. Since Reiche died in December[45] after an illness of six weeks, we may conclude that he was the author of the explanatory material. From this time on the standard of the paper again became lower. It suspended publication during the height of the yellow fever epidemics of 1793, 1798 and 1799. In 1793 both Kämmerer[46] and Steiner, who were its publishers, were attacked by the fever, but fortunately recovered.[47] In 1798 the three Kämmerer brothers, Henrich, Joseph and Friedrich, who were then the publishers, also fell ill with the disease, and two of them, Henrich, the oldest, and Friedrich, the youngest,[48] failed to recover.

When the Kämmerer brothers took charge of it in 1798, they promised to make it strictly non-partisan. At first they published communications from both political parties. They soon, however, commenced to show preference for the Anti-Federalists, probably because the rival Philadelphia German paper, Schweitzer's *Pennsylvanische Correspondenz*, vigorously espoused the cause of Federalism. In 1799 the *Philadelphische Correspondenz* aggressively attacked the Lutheran minister, the Reverend Endresz.[49] This marks the end of the close connection which had up to that time existed between this journal and the Lutheran church.

The paper reached its lowest ebb in March, 1800, when

---

[45] PC₂ 23.

[46] According to the "Geschichte der deutschen Gesellschaft" (p. 501). H. Kämmerer was a prominent member and officer of the "Gesellschaft," was a captain in the Revolutionary War and member of the Pennsylvania Assembly from 1792-1794. He probably died in 1797.

[47] PC₂ 252.

[48] PC₃ 22.

[49] PC₃ 44 ff.

it contained hardly any news or advertisements, but was filled with extracts copied from various German American papers. We may safely assert that the *Philadelphische Correspondenz* was at one period of its existence among the best edited German papers of the post-Revolutionary days, and at another, unquestionably the worst. The limit was reached when the sole proprietor, George Helmbold, Jr.,[50] confessed that he could not write articles in German, but had to hire somebody to translate them for him from English.[51] We can not help wondering how his thrice-a-week edition[52] looked. Unfortunately, or fortunately perhaps, no copies of it have been discovered. When Helmbold took John Geyer[53] into the firm in April, 1800, the paper improved again, if the few copies located give us a fair idea of it. According to McCulloch,[54] the paper was continued by Geyer to August 12, 1812, when its long existence came to an end.

From 1781 to 1785 Steiner's paper had no competitors. In 1785, however, Peter Leibert, a wealthy Dunker, commenced the bi-weekly *Germantauner Zeitung* for his son-in-law, Michael Billmeyer, a Lutheran. Leibert did this in order to have his daughter and his son-in-law near him. He was an old man and intended to retire from active

---

[50] George Helmbold, according to Cist's "Cincinnati Miscellanies" (Vol. I p. 98) published an English paper, the *Tickler*, in 1807 in Philadelphia, and after the War of 1812, the *Independent Balance*. He served as a private in this war.

[51] PC₃ 69.

[52] See bibliography.

[53] John Geyer was born in Philadelphia on April 18, 1778. In 1810 he and Conrad Zentler published *Der americanische Beobachter*. In 1813 he was mayor of Philadelphia. He died in October 1835. (These statements from "Geschichte der deutschen Gesellschaft," p. 482.)

[54] McCulloch's Additional Memoranda, p. 242.

participation in the publication of the paper as soon as Billmeyer should have learned the trade thoroughly.[55]

Having sufficient capital at their command, the new firm immediately became a formidable rival of Steiner. They published the new Lutheran hymnal in 1786.[56] The Pennsylvania Assembly selected them as the German publishers of its proceedings. This met with strong opposition from Steiner, who apparently had a petition circulated in November, 1785, to induce the Assembly to choose another German printer, on the ground that the *Germantauner Zeitung* was not as influential in Philadelphia as the *Philadelphische Correspondenz*.[57] To this Billmeyer replied that, although he had only one hundred and sixty subscribers in the city, his publication had many more readers in the rural districts than Steiner's.[58] It is safe to assume that this statement was entirely true, because the sectarians, most of whom lived in the country, assuredly preferred this paper, since one of its publishers was a Dunker and since its name, *Germantauner Zeitung*, reminded[59] the older ones of Saur's influential paper.[60] Moreover, the firm attempted to make it useful to the farmers by publishing articles[61] on improved agricultural methods.

As agreed upon, Leibert in 1787 severed his connection with the firm which was publishing the newspaper, although he continued to publish books in his own name. The intimate relations of the men did not cease, as is

[55] GZ 27.
[56] GZ 42.
[57] PC 251.
[58] GZ 27.
[59] PC 195.
[60] It, however, voiced none of the peculiar Dunker beliefs such as nonresistance and opposition to higher education.
[61] See GZ₂ 44, 58, GZ 62, 65, 67, 68 et al.

proved by the fact that Billmeyer lived in Leibert's house to the spring of 1789.[62] In 1790 the paper was changed to a weekly and reduced in size. The last copy which I have located bears the date of January 15, 1793.[63]

With the next paper published in the vicinity of Philadelphia, Samuel Saur's *Chesnuthiller Wochenschrift*, I do not need to concern myself here, because it has been discussed at another place. In October, 1797, Heinrich Schweitzer started his semi-weekly *Pennsylvanische Correspondenz* in Philadelphia. Seidensticker[64] says it succeeded Steiner's *Philadelphische Correspondenz*. This is a mistake, since, as we have seen, the latter paper continued into the nineteenth century. The *Pennsylvanische Correspondenz* was strongly Federalist in politics, as is proved by the attacks directed against it in the *Philadelphische Correspondenz*.[65] It was supported by many of the German Lutherans.[66] It is not known how long the paper was published after it was made a weekly in August, 1800. I have been able to find only few accounts of Schweitzer. He was married to Polly Kugler, of Philadelphia, on April 14, 1799,[67] was secretary of the German Society in 1800 and died in 1810.[68]

The real deterioration of the German press commenced when German newspapers began to appear in the inland towns. Since the different localities naturally encouraged their home papers, the Philadelphia papers inevitably lost many country subscribers. With ever-decreasing revenue

---

[62] GZ 110.
[63] See bibliography.
[64] "First Century of German Printing in America," p. 150.
[65] See PCs 66 ff and July 30, 1800.
[66] PCs 67.
[67] PCs 44.
[68] Seidensticker, op. cit., p. 150.

their standards became continually lower. But the inland newspapers were generally just as poor. They were commonly published by men of little education, less wealth and no talent at all. Since the papers presumably had only a limited local circulation, the publishers had great difficulty in avoiding bankruptcy. In spite of this, they might have improved, if the heated politics of 1795-1800 had not caused the establishment, in almost every town, of German organs of the two parties. Thus we find two papers of opposing political opinions in York, Lancaster, Reading and Philadelphia. The result may be imagined. Competition in this case was detrimental to both parties.

Another reason why the German papers did not thrive was Pennsylvania German economy. In 1790 the German publishers of Lancaster complain that, while the Anglo-American press is flourishing, the German American press is losing ground. Although the English papers cost two dollars per year and the German only one dollar, the Germans club together so that two, three or four families get a newspaper in common. If a book costs more than nine pence or one shilling, the Germans will not buy it. The result is that the English publications are superior to the German.[69]

Still another cause of the deterioration of the German papers is probably found in the tendency of the Germans to become anglicized in speech.[70] Since, according to one estimate, only six thousand Germans came to this country between 1765 and 1785,[71] this assimilation gained great impetus. Hence an increasing number of Germans failed to support German newspapers.

[69] NUL 175.
[70] See Chapter V.
[71] GP 10. This estimate is undoubtedly too low. Ten thousand is more nearly correct.

The honor of establishing the first post bellum German paper in the interior of Pennsylvania belongs to the town of Lancaster. On August 8, 1787, the first issue of the *Neue Unpartheyische Lancäster Zeitung* appeared. The publishers were Stiemer, Albrecht and Lahn. In the first number they promise to make the paper of value to the young people by moral and instructive essays. They desire to be non-partisan. They will encourage higher education. They expect to print accounts of European affairs, especially of those of Germany. These promises were fairly well kept at first. The paper became the strong champion of the new Franklin College at Lancaster. It always encouraged religious tolerance. It sturdily urged the adoption of the new Federal Constitution. In addition to this, it occasionally published articles on improved methods of farming.

Anthon Stiemer had begun his apprenticeship with Christoph Saur, the second, and finished it with Carl Cist.[72] In 1783 an Anthon Stiemer was a merchant in Philadelphia.[73] Stiemer was probably the most talented member of the firm, for the paper became noticeably poorer after his death in April, 1788, when he was still less than thirty years of age.

Jacob Lahn was probably the best educated and wealthiest member of the firm. In 1783 he desired to commence a French evening school in Philadelphia.[74] In 1785 he owned a circulating library in that city.[75] He retired from active partnership in the firm in the spring of 1790. After that he conducted a large book store in Lancaster.[76]

[72] McCulloch's Additional Memoranda, p. 190.
[73] PC 109.
[74] PC 124.
[75] PC 217.
[76] NUL 130, 169 ff. 202, 227, 258.

Johann Albrecht, the third member of the firm, had also served his apprenticeship with Saur. He was considered the best pressman in America.[77] In 1788 his firm won the prize offered by the "Pennsylvania Society for the Encouragement of Manufacturing and of the Useful Arts" for the best and finest specimen of a bound book of not less than one hundred and fifty pages, which was printed from type and on paper made in Pennsylvania.[78] When Albrecht became the leading member of the firm the paper lost almost all of its originality. It was already anti-French in 1793. It is unfortunate that no copies of it have been found which were published between the end of 1793 and the beginning of 1798, because it was in this period that the political alignment occurred, which made the German papers of 1798–1800 almost exclusively political in character.

At the beginning of 1798 Johann Albrecht and Company changed the name of the paper to *Der Deutsche Porcupein*. Albrecht frankly said that the purpose of the paper was the same as that of William Cobbett's *Peter Porcupine's Gazette*, namely, to defend the country against the Democrats, Jacobins and disturbers of the peace.[79] Although the change of name created quite a storm of protest, he defended himself by saying that he did not want to use the word "unpartheyische" any longer, because some "unpartheyische" papers had appeared which were an injustice to the name.[80] He probably referred to the Reading *Adler* and to the *York Gazette*. The paper was undoubtedly faithful to the purpose just mentioned.

[77] McCulloch's Additional Memoranda, p. 190.
[78] NUL 68.
[79] DP 1.
[80] DP 2.

For two years it poured forth a perfect stream of coarse abuse on the Anti-federalists, to the exclusion of almost everything else. In this it surpassed all other German Federalist papers which I have read. In 1800, when its name was changed to *Der Americanische Staatsbothe*, its tone became calmer, but the general standard did not improve.

We do not know the exact date when the first opposition paper was launched in Lancaster. Both Seidensticker[81] and Miller[82] say the second German paper in that town was *Der Lancaster Correspondent*. However, I have discovered that an Anti-federalist paper, *Des Landmanns Wochenblatt*, was commenced in February, 1798, and suspended publication on February 19, 1799. Its successor, *Das Lancaster Wochenblatt*, started on February 26, 1799, and had already passed out of existence on May 25, 1799, when *Der Lancaster Correspondent* made its initial appearance.[83] Since no copies of these papers have been located, we know nothing about their characteristics, although we have no reason to doubt that they were almost entirely filled with political news. The publisher of both papers was William Hamilton,[84] who had been publishing an English paper, the *Lancaster Journal*, in Lancaster for a number of years. The editor of the *Landmanns Wochenblatt*, and probably also of the *Lancaster Wochenblatt*, was Conrad Wortmann, a German from the old country.

Christian Jacob Hütter, the publisher of *Der Lancaster Correspondent*, said in the first number of his paper that it would be non-partisan in its news, but that he was proud

---

[81] Seidensticker, op. cit., p. 152.
[82] Daniel Miller's "Early German American Newspaper," p. 47.
[83] See bibliography for further details.
[84] See *Lancaster Journal* of Jan. 27, 1798. Also H 1.

to be an American. "Wir sind Americaner! wir haben die Fackel der Freyheit angezündet!" He did not retain this moderate tone for any length of time. Attacked by Albrecht, Hütter vied with him in vilification. He continued the paper to September 3, 1803. Then he moved[85] to Easton, Northampton County, where he commenced *Der Northampton Correspondent* in 1806, which remained in existence up to 1903. Hütter was born in Saxe-Gotha, Germany, on May 17, 1771, came to America in 1789 and settled in Bethlehem. After he had started the *Northampton Correspondent*, he also made three attempts to publish English papers, *The Pennsylvania Herald and Easton Intelligencer*, *The People's Instructor* and *The Centinel*. During the War of 1812 he was a lieutenant-colonel of the militia. From 1822 to 1825 he was a member of the Pennsylvania House of Representatives.[86]

The second inland town of Pennsylvania which could boast of a German paper was Reading. The first number of the *Neue Unpartheyische Readinger Zeitung* appeared on February 18, 1789. The firm was Johnson, Barton and Jungmann. Johnson was probably Benjamin Johnson, who conducted a hardware store in Reading and sold books.[87] I have been unable to learn anything about Barton. Gottlob Jungmann, who was the only one of the three connected with the firm later than 1793, was undoubtedly the editor of the paper. His opponent, Jacob Schneider of the *Adler*, said[88] that Jungmann in his early years had been a teacher, a musician, a clerk in a store, a

---

[85] See Miller, op. cit., p. 47.

[86] This information about Hütter, I have obtained from Mr. O. L. Fehr of Easton, Pennsylvania, who was the last publisher of *Der Northampton Correspondent*.

[87] NUR 1.

[88] A 57.

weaver, a notorious card player and a soldier, but had never been successful in anything. After discounting Schneider's malice toward Jungmann, we can still believe that he had had a rather checkered career. When the *Readinger Zeitung* had passed out of existence in the first decade of the new century, he started *Der Standhafte Patriot*.[89] I have been unable to ascertain anything about Brückmann, one of Jungmann's later partners. Johann[90] Gruber, who belonged to the firm from June 26, 1793, to December 31, 1794, was born October 31, 1768, at Strasburg, Lancaster County. He was apprenticed at the age of fifteen to Charles Cist to learn the art of printing. After the completion of his apprenticeship his father advised a sea voyage on account of his poor health. In 1791 he went to San Domingo. During his stay there he was engaged as a compositor on a French newspaper. Because of the rebellion which was raging on the island, he was obliged to escape in the disguise of a sailor. After severing relations with Jungmann, he settled at Hagerstown, Maryland, where he started *Die Westliche Correspondenz*.[91] He died at this place on December 29, 1857.

In the first number of the *Neue Unpartheyische Readinger Zeitung* the publishers enumerate sundry advantages which they hope will arise from the publication of the paper. Adults will become more fluent in reading, while children will gladly go to school and learn in order that they may be able to read the paper. Thus the desire for knowledge will grow. Everybody will understand our government better. The people of Berks County will

[89] Daniel Miller, op. cit. p. 57.
[90] For this biography of J. Gruber, I am indebted to Mr. M. A. Gruber, Washington, D. C., a descendant of a collateral branch of the family.
[91] See below.

learn something about the views of their neighbors. They will be able to vote more intelligently. The farmers can read about new methods in farming. Old prejudices and superstitions will pack up and wander over the Blue Mountains. In city and country there will be much reading. The reading of newspapers will lead to the reading of useful books. Schools will be established and a county school at Reading will receive encouragement. The churches will also obtain a fresh stimulus.

Despite the expression of such sanguine hopes, the paper was wretchedly edited. Often more than half of the issue was filled with advertisements. The publishers were frank in confessing that they copied many news items from the *Philadelphische Correspondenz*, the *Germantauner Zeitung*, the *Lancaster Zeitung* and the English papers.[92] Although Jungmann was by no means a talented man, the poverty of the publishers was probably the chief reason for its low standard. When they desired to publish a new edition of the *Marburger Gesangbuch*, they asked the subscribers to pay half of the subscription immediately, so that new type and other necessary materials might be bought.

In the last five years of the century Jungmann also was drawn into the whirlpool of politics. Since he was an ardent Federalist, he lost many readers among his Antifederalist constituency.[93] The loss was accelerated by the appearance of a rival paper which was edited with real ability.

This was the famous Reading *Adler*, the first issue of which (a sample number) appeared on November 29, 1796. It was published by the firm Jacob Schneider and Georg Gerrisch, who in July of that year had started an

[92] NUR 106.
[93] NUR 509.

English paper, *The Impartial Reading Herald*. According to Jungmann,[94] Schneider had been, in the last eight or nine years before he commenced to publish the *Adler*, a teacher, a silversmith, a clockmaker, a miller, a bookbinder, a hotel landlord, the owner of a billiard table, a sign painter, Jungmann's helper, a Lancaster and Reading post rider. Schneider calmly admitted that Jungmann's statements were accurate.[95] The partnership of Schneider and Gerrisch was dissolved when the latter fled from Reading, leaving many debts.[96] Apparently he was also accused of horse stealing, since a Robert Harris offered a reward for the arrest of George Gerrisch, book printer, who had stolen a black mare from him.[97]

The publishers of the paper state that the chief purposes of newspapers are to help social and political life and to disseminate knowledge. They promise to be as impartial as possible.[98] This paper is much superior to the *Readinger Zeitung* in every way. It is unrivaled in its witty and shrewd attacks on its political opponents.[99] Probably the most remarkable feature about the *Adler* is the fact that it was published continuously for one hundred and seventeen years, a record which no other German American paper has ever equaled. It suspended publication in 1913.

For several reasons it is unfortunate that I have been unable to locate more than two issues of the German papers of York County. Since the town of York was situated on the most traveled highway between Pennsylvania and Maryland, it is probable that these papers contained many

---

[94] NUR 467.
[95] A 57.
[96] NUR 467, A 57.
[97] NUR 440.
[98] A 1.
[99] See Chapter VIII.

references to the German newspapers of Maryland, a subject of which we know so little. It is also almost certain that some of the York County newspapers were unusually well edited.

Die Unpartheyische York Gazette, the first German paper in York County, held a position of prominence among the publications of the time. The German Antifederalist papers copied long articles from it and the Federalist papers mentioned it in the most withering terms at their command. All of the German papers of the period of which I have seen copies mentioned it.[100] Even some of the English papers attacked it, as Fenno's *Gazette of the United States* of 1800. There is no doubt that this frequent mention indicates that the *York Gazette* contained many original items, in marked contrast with almost all of the other German sheets of the day. It was probably broad-minded in its religious views. For instance, it defended Governor McKean when he permitted his daughter to marry a Spanish Catholic.[101] It made an exceedingly bold statement for the time when it asserted in Number 213 that no mortal can decide who is right, he who respects neither the Bible nor divine service, or he who does respect them.[102] The publisher of the paper was Solomon Mäyer, who had come to York from Ephrata,[103] Lancaster County, where he had been publishing in partnership with Henry Willcocks an English paper, *The Lancaster County Political Mirror*, in 1793.[104]

The opposition Federalist paper, *Der Volksberichter*,

---

[100] E.g. AS 109, PC₃ 3, NUR 452, DP 19.
[101] PC₃ 61.
[102] AS 119.
[103] AS 112.
[104] NUR 253.

was started in 1799. The editor was the Reverend Görring,[105] of York. It promised to avoid all partisan one-sidedness. Its main aims were to maintain the Christian religion and to give the young people a useful paper. It was to be in reality a religious paper. This emphasis on religion was caused by the feeling that the Anti-federalists were enemies of religion because they supported the doctrines of the French Revolution. The paper was true to its promises. We find that it published an article in defense of religion.[106] It also attacked Logan's proposed school system[107] because the system would eliminate religious instruction from the school room.[108] In 1800 it printed a bitter three-column attack on free-thinking.[109] The publisher, Andrew Billmeyer, according to Seidensticker,[110] was a brother of Michael Billmeyer, the publisher of the *Germantauner Zeitung*.

The York County German paper published at Hanover was probably a supporter of the Federalists, because the name of the publisher, W. D. Lepper, is mentioned by the *Philadelphische Correspondenz* as one of the pall-bearers at the funeral of the semi-weekly *Pennsylvanische Correspondenz*.[111] According to R. G. Thwaites,[112] W. D. Lepper published *Der Patriot am Ohio* in New Lisbon, Ohio, in 1808. This was presumably the same man who had been in Hanover.

There is some doubt about the time when the first Ger-

---

[105] UH 24.
[106] NUR 584.
[107] See Chapter IV.
[108] NUR 602.
[109] AS 119.
[110] op. cit., p. 153.
[111] PC 7-30-1800.
[112] AAS proceedings, 1908-1909, p. 344.

an newspaper was established in Harrisburg. Seidenicker,[113] quoting William H. Egle, says that *Die Unirtheyische Härrisburg Zeitung* was started on March 1, 794, but it seems rather that the first number was issued 1799.[114] The paper favored the Anti-federalists, but as not strongly partisan. It contained much American :ws copied from the Easton, Reading, Lancaster, York, .agerstown, Baltimore, New York, Philadelphia, Charleswn and other papers. The local news was usually colcted in a column, which was headed by a cut of the rising n.

In 1793 Jacob Weygandt began the publication in aston of the *Neuer Unpartheyischer Eastoner Bothe und orthamptoner Kundschafter*. Judging from the one py which I have seen, the paper was not above the aver- ;e standard of the German publications of the period. pparently it supported the Anti-federalists. The publiher,[115] Jacob Weygandt, was born in Germantown on ecember 13, 1742, a son of Palatine immigrants. In 151 the family moved to what is now South Bethlehem, id in 1761 to the vicinity of the present borough of atamy, Northampton County. After having served as ptain in the War for Independence, Weygandt settled at aston, where he commenced the paper mentioned above. 1805 it was succeeded by *Der Eastoner Deutsche Patriot d Landmanns Wochenblatt*, which was discontinued on pril 1, 1814. Weygandt was State Assemblyman from 108 to 1811. He died on July 11, 1828.

The subject of German papers in Maryland is an unex-

---

[13] See op. cit., p. 137.
[14] For fuller details, see my bibliography.
[15] I owe the material for this biographical sketch to the courtesy of :. Ethan Allen Weaver of Germantown, one of Weygandt's descendants.

plored one. Only two copies of the five German papers which are known to have existed in Maryland before 1801 have been located. The names of only three of the five have been definitely established. Absolutely nothing is known of Henry Dulheuer and his Baltimore paper of 1786, except the advertisement in the *Maryland Journal* of June 16, 1786. Matthias Bärtgis, the Frederick publisher, began printing in that town as early as 1774.[116] In 1776 he was also operating a press in Lancaster.[117] We know nothing of the characteristics of his German papers. Johann Gruber's *Westliche Correspondenz* of Hagerstown probably supported the Anti-federalists, because it is called *Die Hägerstauner Demokratische Wochenschrift*.[118] Samuel Saur's Baltimore paper was presumably neutral in the political controversy. Unless Saur completely changed his viewpoint, he certainly did not support the Anti-federalists with their reputation of being free-thinkers.

There were three post-revolutionary publications in Pennsylvania which can hardly be considered newspapers, but which should be discussed briefly, because they were periodical publications issued by the newspaper firms. They were *Der General Post-Bothe,* published in Philadelphia in 1790; the *Philadelphisches Magazin,* published in Philadelphia in 1798; and *Das neue monatliche Readinger Magazin,* published in Reading in 1799. None of them remained in existence more than six months.

The aim of the first publication was to give to the Germans more information about the history and the events of the old world, and also to aid their development in their

---

[116] See Seidensticker, op. cit., p. 87.

[117] Seidensticker, op. cit., p. 95.

[118] NUR 530. Or does this mean that there were two German papers at Hagerstown?

new home. Within a short time, however, the contents of the little semi-weekly publication were composed almost exclusively of a history of the world from the earliest times. Since there were only three hundred and fifty subscribers,[119] the paper was discontinued at the end of June, 1790. The editor, C. C. Reiche, a native of Berlin, had come to America in 1787 or 1788.[120] He had the degree of Master of Arts, having studied at Frankfurt an der Oder, at Halle[121] and in Saxony.[120] He died on December 11, 1790, at the age of fifty.

The Philadelphia magazine and the Reading magazine were published respectively by the publishers of the *Philadelphische Correspondenz* and the Reading *Adler*. The contents of the magazines may be judged from the following table of contents of the first issue of the Reading magazine:[122]

(1) Die Staatsverfassung der vereinigten Americanischen Staaten.
(2) Art Grundbeeren-Brod zu backen.
(3) Kraft des Caffees von Eicheln.
(4) Vom Ackerbau.
(5) Philosophisches Gespräch.
(6) Die Edelfrau unter Mördern.
(7) Charlotte Ormond.
Poesie.
(8) Auf die Zerstörung der Bastille.
(9) Das fromme Mädchen.
(10) Die unzeitige Kur.
(11) Lasz der Jugend Sonnenschein, etc.

[119] GP 45.
[120] PC₂ 23.
[121] GP. 20.
[122] A 114 ff.

(12) Anecdoten.
(13) Politisches Register.

For a complete statistical presentation of the newspapers rapidly surveyed in this introductory chapter, the reader is referred to the tables and bibliography at the close of this investigation.

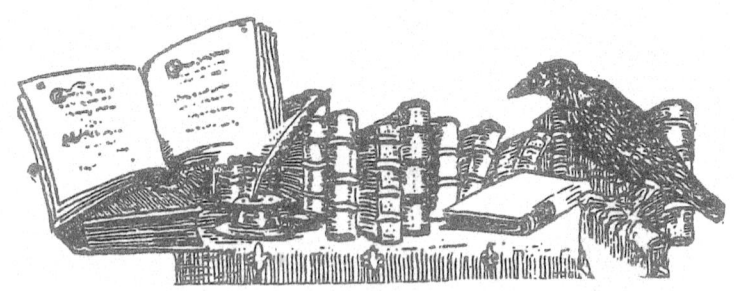

CHAPTER II.

THE RELIGION AND THE RELIGIOUS DENOMINATIONS OF THE PENNSYLVANIA GERMANS.

SINCE many of the Germans who came to the New World in the eighteenth century left their native country because they were not allowed the liberty of worshiping their God in their own way, it is not at all surprising that religion was one of the dominating factors of Pennsylvania German civilization throughout the entire century. In fact we find that the various religious denominations or their pastors exerted a very powerful influence on almost all of the educational ventures, on a great many charitable undertakings and even on the politics of the period.[123] The Dunkers, the Mennonites, the Seventh Day Dunkers, the Reformed, the Lutherans, the Moravians, the Catholics, the Schwenkfelders and the Separatists are mentioned in the newspapers, the last two, however, receiving only passing mention.[124]

The Dunkers and the Mennonites have many beliefs in common. Saur's paper, as the great Dunker organ, is the

---

[123] For a discussion of the activities of the ministers in these fields, see Chapters III, IV, VIII.

[124] The English and German Quakers are not differentiated in the papers.

only one which gives us a fair idea of these sects. They believed that conversion was a personal experience.[125] They had very little faith in the value of a physician whom Saur at one time called "Doc Thor."[126] They were opposed to lawyers and refused to institute legal proceedings. In 1746 Saur gave an account[127] of a law suit over poor fences between a minister and a layman. He declared that poor fences were often the beginning of disputes, and that the lawyers laughed at the Germans for working so hard and then willingly sacrificing their savings for such slight reasons. No Dunker, he added, as long as he remained a member of the denomination, ever started a law suit against any person. In describing the terrible conditions of the immigrants in 1745, Saur in his quaint phraseology said, "Solte der alte Cain zu unserer Zeit einen perfecten Lawyer und Geld genug haben, er solte beweisen, er hätte den Abel nicht einmal gesehen."[128] In 1760 the second Saur reported that when Georgia was settled it was decided that no negroes, no lawyers and no rum should be brought into the new colony. If these three things had been excluded by law from Pennsylvania at the time of its settlement, many godless actions would have been prevented.[129]

Another noteworthy characteristic of these so-called sectarians was their policy of non-resistance. They desired to live at peace with everybody, with friends as well as hostile neighbors. In 1748 Saur announced[130] that he had published four articles proving that war, robbery, murder, revenge and defense were un-Christian. Several years

[125] S 79.
[126] S 81.
[127] S 77.
[128] S 55.
[129] S 3-28-60.
[130] S 92.

later[131] he reported that the constable of a certain township had selected a one-armed man as his assistant, because the inhabitants required no strong man to preserve order, all of them being Quakers and Mennonites. Since the sectarians believed in a literal interpretation of the Biblical command, "Love your enemies, and pray for them which persecute you," they naturally were opposed to all wars and to all military preparations even if for defense only. Saur's activity during the French and Indian War will be discussed in another connection,[132] but several instances may here be introduced to show his hostility to "militarism." In 1748 he explained that the difference between a privateer and a pirate consisted simply in this, that the former committed robbery and murder sanctioned by the government, while the latter committed them without such sanction; but, he added, both were alike in eternity.[133] Two months later he announced that five companies of volunteer militia had been mustered out of service and that they could not expect any reward either from God or from men.[134] Samuel Saur published long articles in his *Chesnuthiller Wochenschrift* in order to prove by the Bible that war was contrary to God's will and was the result of sin.[135]

This attitude toward war produced much trouble between these sects and their neighbors. In the fall of 1757 some Dunkers who lived on an advanced frontier line in Virginia were massacred by the Indians.[136] Since they had not made any preparations to defend themselves against the hostile Indians who were known to be in the vicinity,

[131] S 142.
[132] See Chapter VIII.
[133] S 100.
[134] S 102,
[135] CW 122, 125, 126, 129, 134, 137.
[136] S 213.

the English suspected them of treason and consequently gave them no military protection. The Indians, on the other hand, naturally regarded them as enemies, because they were white men living in an English colony. Thus, misunderstood by both parties, they fell as martyrs to their convictions. In the next year the aged Saur was summoned before General Forbes because he was accused of having printed something unfavorable to the English government.[137]

The newspapers contain very little about the famous Seventh Day Dunkers of the Ephrata cloister, a group of people which has been well described by Seidensticker, Sachse and others. On June 23, 1743, when the governor of the province visited the cloister, the brothers and the sisters sang in a four part chorus. On this occasion the governor and his party also viewed the rare pictures in the cloister.[138] In 1746 five members were compelled to leave the monastery because they had bought a bell without the consent of the "Father." At about the same time the others closed the sawmill and the papermill which they operated, and disposed of their cows, oxen, horses, wagons, clocks and bells. They also refused to buy and sell any more wheat and linseed. All these changes were made because it had been rumored that the cloister people were becoming mere merchants.[139] When Conrad Beissel, the founder and leader of the community, was buried in 1768, more than seven hundred people attended the funeral.[140]

Although the Mennonites and the Dunkers attempted to live at peace with all men, Saur's newspaper never

[137] S 219.
[138] S 49.
[139] S 70.
[140] M 339.

neglected to give accounts of the dissensions which arose in other denominations and to describe the shameful actions of some of their ministers.[141] He portrayed a deplorable state of affairs in the ministerial ranks of the Lutherans and the Reformed. Unquestionably he did an injustice to these denominations. He may not have printed any false accounts about them, but he certainly, to a large extent, neglected mentioning the good qualities of the Lutherans, the Reformed and the Moravians—a fact which must be kept in mind.

The Lutherans and the Reformed, the two largest German denominations, always lived in harmony in America. Although to a certain extent differing in doctrine, the difference between the two denominations was not so great as between them and the sectarians. The two denominations insisted on an educated clergy and were not averse to military service. Since it was almost impossible to secure a sufficient number of educated ministers of any standing from the old country, Pennsylvania became the gathering place of clergymen who could not obtain charges in Germany because of immoral conduct. The pious German settlers, eager for regular ministers, often elected the first educated man who came to their church, without asking for certificates or recommendations. Although a warning[142] was sent out from Lancaster in 1750 to the various churches that they should select no minister without proper credentials, conditions did not improve and Saur continued to find many justifiable reasons for attacking the ministerial failings. As early as 1744 he attacked the Lutherans because they wanted to exclude all non-University men from

---

[141] We may almost term his publication a Dunker missionary paper.
[142] S 124.

the ministry.¹⁴³ He said such action was contrary to the charter of Pennsylvania. The next year, when some ministers asserted that his edition of the Bible was not correct, he retorted that they made this charge because he had accused them of adultery.¹⁴⁴ He added that they might consider themselves fortunate for his having refused to institute a law suit. In 1746 his paper charged the Reformed minister of Lancaster, the Reverend Caspar Schnorr, with having been so intoxicated as to fall from his horse.¹⁴⁵ Subsequently, when this minister was compelled to resign on account of lying, drunkenness and adultery,¹⁴⁶ he began to preach at other places, denying the accusations until Conrad Weiser and others proved them against him. Saur attacked the Lutheran ministers as well as the Reformed. In 1753 he printed a communication charging the Reverend Andrä, the Lutheran minister of the old Goshenhoppen church, with being a drunkard and an adulterer.¹⁴⁷ He grew sarcastic when announcing in 1754 the death of Reverend Andrä, who had in the meantime taken charge of the Germantown Lutheran Church. He said the late minister was a poet, especially when drunk.¹⁴⁸ In giving an account of three ministers who were continually fighting, viz., Reverend Jonas Witzler of Germantown, Reverend Wartemann of Reading and Reverend Ohrendorff of Tolpehocken, Saur said he was publishing this story in the hope that it would teach his countrymen the

---

[143] S 49.
[144] S 63. Although the denominations of these ministers are not specifically stated, they were undoubtedly Lutherans and Reformed.
[145] S 70.
[146] S 113.
[147] S 7-1-53.
[148] S 164.

danger of selecting as a minister any rascal who happened to come from Germany.[149]

Saur seemed to take especial delight in giving full space to the church quarrels. In 1749[150] the German Reformed congregation of Philadelphia refused to elect as their permanent minister the Reverend Schlatter, one of the organizers of the German Reformed Church of America. A few months later, when the majority of the congregation chose the Reverend Steiner, Reverend Schlatter refused to leave.[151] Saur gave a most amusing account[152] of the church services at which both ministers attempted to win possession of the field. On January 28, 1750, after Steiner had commenced to preach, Schlatter entered the church and interrupted him by saying, "Ich gebiete euch an Gottes Staat, dasz ihr von meinem Stuhl herunter kommen solt." Saur's narrative continues with the statement that Steiner did not accept Schlatter to be God's ambassador and remained standing. When Schlatter, having taken his position in front of the pulpit, attempted to begin preaching, Steiner's adherents began to sing the one hundred and fortieth psalm, "Errett' mich, o mein lieber Herre von Menschen arg und bös." When Steiner began the Lord's prayer, Schlatter's party interrupted him in the middle of it by starting a hymn. Thereupon Schlatter tried to speak again, but the opposing party sang "Sie dencken nur auf Buben Stücken." In this way the Steiner party sang six times and the adherents of Schlatter eighteen times during the course of the next two hours. A month later a neutral board of six persons, chosen by the two

[149] S 11-1-53.
[150] S 8-1-49.
[151] S 116.
[152] S 2-1-50.

sides, decided that the Schlatter party might retain the church, but that they would be obliged to pay the debts contracted by the other party. This board, as Saur says approvingly, contained no judge, no lawyer and no minister, but was composed of five Quakers and one High Church man.[153]

We should notice, however, that Saur never attacked Schlatter's private life. When the latter set sail for Germany early in 1751, Saur said his great mistake had been in not taking his elders and his deacons more completely into his confidence. Saur was Schlatter's bitter opponent in the charity school movement of 1754–1757,[154] because the former believed that the schools had been organized for the express purpose of anglicizing the Germans. When Schlatter was appointed chaplain of the fourth batallion in 1757, Saur commented, "Wan er auch zugleich ihr Seel Sorger seyn will, und sie in Christliche Zucht und Ordnung bringen: Oder in die Nachfolge Jesu einführen will, so hat er gewiszlich ein recht schweres Amt auf sich genommen."[155]

Saur also gave an account of the schism in the Lutheran church of Germantown in 1753 when the congregation dismissed Reverend Handschuh by a vote of two hundred to fifteen.[156] As the minority followed the minister, Saur exclaimed that one part of the congregation had the minister and the other part had the church building.[157] Later in the year the infamous Reverend Andrä, mentioned above, was elected pastor by the majority, while the minor-

[153] S 118.
[154] See Chapter IV.
[155] S 4–16–57.
[156] S 154.
[157] S 4–1–53.

ity began to plan the erection of another church.[158] Gradually the church and ministerial scandals ceased. Miller announced one occurrence in his *Staatsbote* of 1763, viz., that Reverend Friedrich Rothenbühler had been deposed by the German Reformed congregation of Philadelphia.[159] Although this is the last removal of which I have found an account in the newspapers, we may well believe that dissensions still occurred sporadically.

Although Saur devoted much space to the scandals and dissensions in the Lutheran and the Reformed churches, he also expressed a desire for more tolerance among the various sects and denominations. On April 29, 1749, a Reformed minister, Reverend Johann Boehm, died. Since no minister of the denomination could arrive in time to conduct the funeral services, the Mennonite "teacher" or minister, Martin Kolb, preached the sermon. Saur commented[160] on this as follows: "Wan solches und dergleichen ohne Not gebräuchlich und gemein wird, so wird aller partheyliche Neid und Wiederigkeit ein Ende nehmen. Wie schön wirds ein mahl seyn wenn nur ein Hirt und nur eine Herde seyn wird? Bisz dahin Geduld." Again in 1753 he praised the Reformed minister, the Reverend Zubly, of Charlestown, South Carolina, who was holding evangelistic services in Philadelphia and was invited by all the churches, the two divisions of the Presbyterians, the Lutherans, the Reformed of both parties, the Baptists, the Separatists and the Schwenkfelders. Eleven ministers heard him at one time. Saur could not refrain from adding that it was fortunate that the Reverend Zubly did not find it necessary to study his sermons or to write them out,

[158] S 156.
[159] M 83.
[160] S 108.

because he would have had no time to do it. He did not go to places where he would be able to rest six days and twenty hours per week.[161]

As I have mentioned before, the Lutherans and the Reformed demanded specially educated ministers. This rule, so bitterly opposed by Saur, caused these two denominations to become the leaders in the social development of the Pennsylvania Germans. Their ministerial leaders, as well-educated men, saw distinctly the crying need of better educational facilities. We find them supporting and encouraging every movement for the establishment of colleges for the Germans.[162] They also often formed the connecting link between the Germans and the other colonists in the political field.[163] They were likewise the founders of numerous charitable organizations.[164]

The patriarch of the Lutheran church in America, Heinrich Melchior Mühlenberg, who had been himself a student at Göttingen and Halle,[165] sent his three sons to the latter place to study for the ministry. Two of them, Peter and Friedrich August, later left the ministry to serve their country in other fields.[166] The third one, Heinrich, became pastor of the Lutheran church at Lancaster and, in 1787, the first president of Franklin College at that place.[167] Two Lutheran ministers of Philadelphia, the Reverend J. C. Kunze and the Reverend J. H. C. Helmuth, were the moving spirits of the German department of the University of Pennsylvania from 1780 to 1786.[167]

[161] S 157.
[162] See Chapter IV.
[163] See Chapter VIII.
[164] See Chapter III.
[165] See "Hallesche Nachrichten."
[166] See Chapter VIII.
[167] See Chapter IV.

These same men had charge of Steiner's paper for about two years.[166] The Reverend Friedrich Valentin Melsheimer, a Lutheran minister, was chosen professor of Latin, Greek and German at Franklin College in 1787.[167] Reverend Görring, the Lutheran minister at York, was editor of the York *Volksberichter*.[168] These men, in addition to Reverend Handschuh, who was teacher of French from 1755 to 1758 at the academy which later became the University of Pennsylvania, and who was also for a time editor of Franklin and Armbrüster's *Philadelphische Zeitung*,[168] gave the Lutherans a most predominating influence in the development of the Pennsylvania Germans. The Reformed ministers apparently did not exert so much influence. Besides the Reverend Schlatter's interest in the charity schools, I have found only one minister of the denomination who was prominent either as an educator or as a statesman. This was the Reverend William Händel, the Reformed pastor at Lancaster, who was elected vice-president of Franklin College at the time of its organization in 1787.[169]

The Lutherans and the Reformed erected many church buildings in the last two decades of the century. The congregations inserted advertisements in the newspapers announcing the laying of corner stones or the dedication services of the churches. Thus in the nine years between June, 1789, and June, 1798, the *Neue Unpartheyische Readinger Zeitung* announced the building of five Lutheran, two Reformed and four union (Lutheran and Reformed) churches, most of which were located in Berks County.[170]

---

[168] See Chapter I.
[169] See Chapter IV.
[170] It must be remembered that the erection of these churches does not necessarily indicate the organization of new congregations. The old congregations were simply building new places of worship.

The activities of the Zion Lutheran congregation of Philadelphia deserve special mention, because this congregation not only built one of the finest church edifices in America, but also displayed an active interest in charity and education. From a full-page article by F. A. Mühlenberg in the *Philadelphische Correspondenz* of January 13, 1795, we learn that the congregation was organized in 1742, and that the first church building (Saint Michael's Church) was erected shortly afterwards. By 1760 the congregation also possessed a schoolhouse, a parsonage and a cemetery. In 1766 the second church building (Zion's Church) was begun. Its dimensions were one hundred and eight feet in length and eighty feet in width. This was the building which was called in 1790 "one of the finest, if not the finest, building in Philadelphia."[171] It was dedicated June 25, 1769.[172] The land on which the church was built cost fifteen hundred pounds, while the church itself was erected at a cost of eleven thousand pounds.[173] In 1778 the British used the building as a hospital. After they left the city the congregation was obliged to spend two thousand pounds to repair the interior of the church, including the installation of new pews. Between 1780 and 1790 much money was spent by the church for charitable purposes.[174]

In 1790 David Tanneberg,[175] of Lititz, Lancaster County, Pennsylvania, built for the church the largest pipe organ in America.[176] The organ was twenty-four feet long, eight feet wide and twenty-seven feet high. Standing

---

[171] NUL 168, PC₂ 4.
[172] M 389.
[173] A communication in PC₂ 366 says the total cost was 15,000 pounds.
[174] See Chapters III and IV.
[175] See Chapter VII.
[176] This detailed description is found in NUL 168, PC₂ 4.

in front of it, the spectator could see more than one hundred pipes, some of which were sixteen feet high. There were almost two thousand pipes in the interior. On the top of the organ was a representation of the sun rising out of the clouds and dividing them with its rays. To the right and the left of the sun were two eagles which were flying toward it and bearing scrolls with the inscriptions, "Die auf den Herrn harren, fahren auf wie die Adler!" Beside each of the eagles there was an angel. The one carried the gospel and the other the sealed book, while both had trumpets in their hands. The cost of the entire organ was three thousand five hundred pounds.[177] It was dedicated on Sunday and Monday, October 10 and 11, 1790. For this occasion the Reverend Helmuth, the pastor, had composed special and suitable hymns and had them printed.

In the next years the congregation built a schoolhouse in the Northern Liberties of Philadelphia, which was also to be used as a place of worship by the old and infirm of that vicinity.[177] On December 26, 1794, the large church with its magnificent organ was destroyed by fire.[178] The following poem appeared in the *Philadelphische Correspondenz* of January 9, 1795, under the title of "Gedanken auf den Ruinen der Zions-Kirche":

>Hier weine segensvolle Güsse,
> Betrübtes Herz! auf Zion hin;
>Denn hier betreten deine Füsse
> Den Tempel Gottes im Ruin;
>Wo sonst des Himmels Quelle flosz.
>Und dich mit Heil und Trost begosz!

[177] PC, 370.
[178] PC, 366.

Wie oft empfand ich hier die Liebe,
   Des, der die ganze Welt erschuf,
Ich fühlte seine Gnadentriebe
   Bey seiner Knechte mildem Ruf,
Und weinend schwur ich ihm allein,
Und ihm, auf ewig treu zu seyn.

Holdselig Wort von Jesu Leiden!
   Wie rührend fülltest du mein Herz!
Du banntest alle eiteln Freuden,
   Du scheuchtest allen Seelen Schmerz
Wenn Jesu Knecht aus Jesu Buch,
Dich thränend hier im Munde trug.

O H———h,[179] deine holde Stimme,
Die kindlich, doch mit Ernste rief;
Die risz mich hier vom starren Grimme
   Des Feindes, da ich ruhig schlief;
Die trieb mich erst zum Beten an—
Gott lohne dich, O Gottesmann!

Und du gelasz' ner Diener Gottes,
   O Sch———![180] beruhigtest den Geist,
Da mich der Greuel alles Spottes,
   Oft tief in Traurigkeit verweis't:
An dieser Stelle gab dein Mund
Der Seele Trost und fester Grund.

Hier war's, wo du mir von der Krone,
   Die unaufhörlich ewig währt,
O theurer K———e![181] dem zu Lohne,
   Der Jesu dient, so schön belehrt,
Dasz ich die Sünde nun verschwur,
Und thränend rief: Die Krone nur!

Und diese sonst so frohe Stelle,
   Wo jeder Segen sich ergosz;
Wo Jesu Christi Liebes-Quelle
   Vom Munde seiner Diener flosz;
Wo mich Gebet, Music, Gesang,
So oft zu süszen Thränen zwang!

---

[179] Reverend Handschuh.
[180] Reverend Schulze.
[181] Reverend Kunze.

> Die ist dahin—Ach, meine Sünden!
>   Die halfen auch den grausen Brand
> Des Zornes Himmels zu entzünden,
>   Der diesen Tempel uns entwand!
> Ich schwur so oft ihm treu zu seyn
> Und blieb es nicht—O Jammer, Nein!
>
> Doch, Herr! du zürnest stets voll Liebe,
>   Du willst wir sollen glücklich seyn,
> Du folgtest deinem Liebestriebe,
>   Und schlugest hier mit Ruthen drein:
> Drum, Herr! wir kommen nun heran,
> Wir hören dich—O nimm uns an!

For almost two years the Lutherans held their services in the Reformed church of Philadelphia. On November 18, 1796, the officers of the Lutheran church publicly thanked the Reformed congregation for their kindness. The address and the response are printed in the *Philadelphische Correspondenz* of November 22, 1796. From this account we learn that the erection of the new church was so far advanced that the services would be held in it on and after November 27. We learn further that the Reformed congregation had raised a subscription of several hundred pounds to aid the Lutherans, although they themselves were planning to build a large, comfortable and expensive schoolhouse.

It is unfortunate for my purpose that there are comparatively few references to the Moravians in the newspapers. From other sources,[182] however, we know that the Moravian leader, Count Nicholas von Zinzendorf, came to America in 1741 and attempted the following year to unite all the German religious denominations of the province into one body. Unfortunately only one newspaper copy of these years has been located.

[182] For example, Faust's " German Element in the U. S.," Vol. I, p. 126.

The Moravians always insisted that they were Lutherans, while the regular Lutheran ministers refused to acknowledge them as such, with the result that acrimonious disputes arose. In 1745 and 1746 the Lutheran congregation at Lancaster was served by the Reverend Nyberg, a native of Sweden, who exhibited strong Moravian sympathies. In the ensuing law suit Nyberg's adherents were defeated and were compelled to relinquish the church edifice to the orthodox Lutherans.[183] Before the case had been decided Heinrich Melchior Mühlenberg preached in the church, although, according to his opponents,[184] he had previously promised not to do so. His friends, the deacons and elders of the church, however, replied that he conducted services in the church at the special request of the church members.[185] In the Tulpehocken Lutheran church a somewhat similar dispute occurred in 1747.[186] Because the Moravians did not refuse to bear arms and to institute law suits, Saur attacked them in his paper whenever the opportunity offered. In 1746 he claimed[187] that the fact that they participated in wars in Germany proved that they were no Christians. In 1750 he reported that they were now divided into three groups, those that had previously left the denomination, those that were put under the ban, and the Count with his three brethren, who were to be considered the real congregation of the Saviour.[188]

The sect was famous for its educational and missionary zeal. They established elementary schools at various places in the rural districts before 1750. For instance, in

[183] S 68.
[184] S 70.
[185] S 71.
[186] S 87.
[187] S 71.
[188] S 2-1-50.

1745 or 1746 they opened one at *Falckeners Schwamm*, near Philadelphia.[189] After the war they had an academy for girls at Bethlehem and one for boys at Nazareth.[190] In 1790 they were conducting an academy for girls in Philadelphia.[191] The Moravian minister of Lancaster took part in the dedication exercises of Franklin College in 1787,[200] thus giving additional proof that the denomination was interested in encouraging higher education among the Germans. We learn but little of the Moravian missionary endeavors from the newspapers. When Kammerhof, one of the Moravian leaders, died in Bethlehem in 1751, Saur declared that he had attempted to win the good will of the Indians by presenting silver armbands to their chiefs and by erecting a blacksmith shop for them.[192] In 1755, during the French and Indian War, the Moravians' little missionary settlement at Gnadenhütten, situated about thirty miles north of Bethlehem on the Lehigh River, was attacked and burned to the ground by hostile Indians.[193] The natives, however, were usually well disposed toward the Moravians. For instance, a body of Iroquois chiefs and warriors on their way to Philadelphia stopped at Bethlehem on March 9, 1792. On the following day they were welcomed by the members of the "Society for the Spreading of the Gospel among the Heathen." Two persons, a man and a woman, addressed the Indians, and two chiefs responded.[194]

In one respect at least the Moravians were similar to the Baptists of the Ephrata community. They also oper-

---

[189] S 71.
[190] See Chapter IV.
[191] NUR 72.
[192] S 132.
[193] S 12-1-55, S 187, 188.
[194] CW 72, GZ₁ 93, NUL 253.

ated mills and kept cattle. After the Gnadenhütten massacre in 1755 it was reported that six hundred persons in Bethlehem and two hundred orphans in Nazareth had been obtaining most of their bread, butter and meat from the destroyed settlement.[195] In 1766 an advertisement appeared in the papers announcing that the Bethlehem mills for the preparation of hemp and millet and for oil pressing were now in operation, and that those for making bran, barley, groats and oatmeal, and for grinding spelt would be completed during the course of the summer.[196]

In the eighteenth century the German Catholics in Pennsylvania were numerically unimportant. In 1757 they numbered only about three thousand; that is, approximately three per cent. of the total number of Germans.[197] As we shall see in a later chapter,[198] they planned to open a German academy in Philadelphia in 1796. In the last decade of the century the denomination erected a church in Reading, the corner stone of which was laid on August 17, 1791.[199] The dedication services were held on April 28, 1793.[200]

The foregoing facts sufficiently illustrate the deep-rooted religious spirit of the Pennsylvania Germans. Additional evidence can be found in numerous papers. For example, beginning with March 22, 1768, Henrich Miller usually published one or more poems in his paper every week. It is significant that many of them were of a religious nature. The post bellum papers which conducted such a "Dichter-Stelle" also favored poems with religious themes.

[195] S 187.
[196] M 217.
[197] S 184.
[198] See Chapter IV.
[199] NUR 130.
[200] NUR 218.

As may be imagined, free-thinkers and atheists were monstrous creatures in the eyes of these pious Germans. I have found no record that any of the colonial German immigrants were unbelievers. After the war the Federalist publishers sometimes attacked their Anti-federalist opponents, claiming that they were free-thinkers and deists.[201] However, instead of proving that the Germans were losing their simple faith, these attacks simply show how detestable unbelief was to the rank and file of them. There is hardly any doubt that the Federalists emphasized the well-known deistical tendencies of some of the Anti-federalist leaders (*e.g.*, Jefferson) for the purpose of discrediting the party among the Germans. In fact, there are not half a dozen cases of so-called heresy among the Pennsylvania Germans mentioned in the eighteenth century German American papers. Probably the only conspicuous case is the one recorded in Dauphin County in 1799.[202] Andreas Kraus, who had been in this country for only a short time, was convicted of blasphemy by the Dauphin County court. He confessed that he had said, "Christus ist ein verdammt Hurenkind und wann Christus der Sohn Gottes ist, so hat Gott mit seiner Tochter gehuret."

In common with many colonists of other nationalities, the Germans were superstitious. Many of them believed in spooks and witches and had great faith in the efficacy of pow-wowing. These superstitions were vigorously attacked by the newspapers and the better educated people. In 1768[203] Henrich Miller ridiculed the story that a woman who had been buried for sixteen weeks had appeared again on earth in order to tell the living that she

---

[201] *e.g.*, AS 119.
[202] DP 92.
[203] M 335.

had not been buried like her forefathers. The students of the German department of the University of Pennsylvania satirized in a dialogue the belief in witches and spooks.[204] The Lancaster and the Reading papers frequently published articles attacking the prevalent superstitions.[205] For instance, the *Neue Unpartheyische Readinger Zeitung* of March 18, 1789, related the story of a man who was cheated by a certain person who pretended he could cure the man's horse by means of pow-wowing. Despite all these attempts to teach the Germans the folly of such beliefs, it is apparent that the efforts were not entirely successful, for many rural Pennsylvania Germans still retain their belief in spirits, witches and pow-wowing.

With a deeply religious spirit and a strong inclination toward superstition, we might expect to find extreme religious intolerance among the Pennsylvania Germans. This is not the case, however. As we have seen, even in the period between 1740 and 1760 there were men who desired a closer union of all Protestant denominations, in spite of the fact that the various sects were often opposed to one another. The petty antagonisms had largely vanished before the last decade of the century. Then the Moravians began to work in coöperation with the Lutherans and the Reformed, who had always lived in amity and harmony. When the Moravians dedicated the new organ which had been built for their church at Lancaster, the closing services were held in the Lutheran church of that place.[206] Whether the Mennonites and Dunkers were ever close friends of the other Protestant bodies is very doubtful.

[204] PC 182.
[205] See NUL 52, 107, 130, NUR 1, 22, 47, 184, et al.
[206] DP 56.

Religion and Religious Denominations. 57

Although complete toleration had not been achieved at the end of the century, the *Neue Unpartheyische Lancäster Zeitung* in 1788[207] formulated the rule that a man should be allowed to think in peace about God as he pleased, but that he should not be permitted to publish his thoughts if he was a free-thinker. We could hardly imagine Saur or even Miller making such a liberal concession.

[207] NUL 43.

CHAPTER III.

CHARITIES AND HUMANITARIAN ORGANIZATIONS.

THERE was nothing that redounded more to the honor of the Pennsylvania Germans than their unstinted liberality toward those in need or distress. When the call for help arose, all denominations and classes forgot their trivial jealousies and vied with each other in alleviating the sufferings of the unfortunate. They not only gave of their own possessions, but also tried to remedy the causes of the distress.

Almost from the beginning of German immigration to the New World the sufferings of the poorer class were apparent. The second number of Franklin's *Philadelphische Zeitung* of 1732 printed an account of the trial of a ship captain charged with the murder of two German emigrants from the Palatinate. Although he was acquitted, there must have been some cause for complaint about the treatment which the Germans received at the hands of the captains, even at the time when the number of immigrants was still comparatively small.

When it was discovered that many of the poor German peasants could be persuaded to come to America, large numbers of men proceeded to the old country to induce others to leave their homes. These agents, who were known as "newlanders," generally received a commission from the ship companies for every person they succeeded in bringing on shipboard. In 1749 Saur said it was reported that the newlanders received half a doubloon[208] for each passenger.[209] Since many of the agents and ship captains were in the business only to make money, they were utterly unscrupulous, and deceived and cheated the ignorant and confiding peasants whenever possible. The newlanders often pretended that they were rich merchants in Philadelphia and possessed vessels of their own, or that they had houses in Germantown and farms in the country.[210] The Germans were thus led to believe that the newlanders' representatives would meet them in America and would offer them the opportunity of earning sufficient money to pay for their passage. Eager to arrive in the country where everybody was free and wealthy, they went aboard the ships often without even signing a contract.

The long voyage in the sailing vessels, which was tedious and uncomfortable even when conditions were favorable, became for the German emigrants often a veritable martyrdom. The conditions pictured in Saur's paper are almost beyond human comprehension. The overcrowding of the ships, the unsanitary conditions and the insufficient food for the passengers frequently caused the vessels to become charnel houses. On one ship four hundred persons set sail from Europe in the fall of 1743. On the voyage insufficient rations were distributed. Those who desired more food were compelled to buy it from the crew. Since many of the passengers were too poor to do this, they starved to death. On one occasion, when a starving man begged for a little flour, his sack was filled with sand and coal. When

[208] A doubloon—five dollars.
[209] S 112.
[210] S 113.

the vessel arrived at Philadelphia a few more than fifty persons were alive.[211] It was estimated that two thousand Germans died on the voyage to America in 1749.[212] In one case the passengers were not permitted to land immediately, because the ship was full of a disease which had killed half of the immigrants.[213] On June 5, 1752, a ship anchored at Philadelphia with nineteen Germans on board, the miserable remnant of two hundred who had embarked in Europe.[214] Such conditions sometimes drove the passengers to mutiny.[215]

When the Germans arrived in America their condition was frequently not much improved. If they were poor or had no well-to-do friends, they were compelled to sell themselves for a number of years to people who in return paid their passage money. This system of redemptioning, as it was called, was in itself not particularly unjust, but so many abuses arose that it became a public scandal. In the first place, many Germans, as mentioned before, came to America in the belief that they would be met by the representatives of the newlanders, who would furnish them opportunities for work, so that they could earn the expenses of the voyage in a short time. When they arrived they were obliged to sell themselves to people who were utter strangers to them. This sudden transition from independence to servitude undoubtedly created unspeakable hardship. The time of servitude was often considerably lengthened because the survivors had to pay the passage money of those who died at sea. They were at times required to

---

[211] S 55.
[212] S 2-1-50.
[213] S 112.
[214] S 145.
[215] S 112.

pay even for the food which the dead would have bought.[216] Sometimes the captains put into a southern port, where they could sell the passengers into a servitude of four or five years instead of landing them at Philadelphia, where many of them had friends willing to pay the expenses of the voyage.[217] Many chests containing the personal property of the immigrants were broken open and rifled while at sea,[218] so that even those who had some possessions when they embarked found themselves destitute on their arrival. One of the most deplorable aspects of the system of redemptioning in the early days was the breaking up of families. Children of a tender age were sold by unscrupulous captains without the knowledge of their parents, who in some cases were sick on board the ship. In Saur's paper of November 16, 1745, for instance, there were two advertisements by persons desiring to know the whereabouts of their children, who had been sold without their consent or knowledge.[219]

In order to better the lot of these German immigrants, the older Christoph Saur used all the influence which he possessed as publisher of a widely read paper. As we have seen, he revealed prevalent conditions in long articles. It was in one of these accounts[220] that he used the sentence quoted in the preceding chapter, "Solte der alte Cain zu unserer Zeit einen perfecten Lawyer und Geld genug haben,

---

[216] S 55, S 112.

[217] S 112.

[218] S 114.

[219] Not all of the German immigrants were badly treated during the voyage. For instance, in 1749, Saur said concerning the passengers of three ships which had just arrived from Rotterdam, "Sie sind auch menschlich gehalten worden." In 1753 he praised the owners of a ship who had strictly observed their contract.

[220] S 55.

er solte beweisen, er hätte den Abel nicht einmal gesehen." He said this in connection with a complaint that it was very difficult to obtain justice for the wretched immigrants. Again and again[221] Saur emphasized the necessity of having written contracts. In 1749 he advised the Germans in America to write to their friends in Germany who intended to emigrate and to inform them what they should do for their own protection.

His unrelenting crusade against the unscrupulous exploiters of the Germans was unquestionably one of the principal causes which in the winter of 1749–1750 finally moved the Quaker Assembly of Pennsylvania to enact laws which were intended to check the evil. One law[222] forbade the overcrowding of ships. By its provisions every passenger was entitled to a sleeping place which was at least six feet long and two feet wide. If the captain failed to observe this order, he was fined ten pounds for each passenger who did not have the legal amount of room. Half of this fine was given to the passenger and the remainder to the trustees of Province Island, which was used for the accommodation of sick immigrants. Philadelphia inspectors were ordered to examine the ships on arrival. The ship captains were required to make an inventory of the property of those who had died during the voyage.

Although Saur was pleased with this law, he immediately recognized the inadequacy of its provisions. In the issue of his paper which contained an account of the law he advised the Germans to make contracts with the captains so that the latter would be compelled to take care of their personal property, to bring them to the destination agreed upon and to provide berths for them in which they would

---

[221] S 112, 2-1-50, 1-1-55.
[222] S 2-1-50.

be able to sit up. Saur also urged the immigrants to demand receipts if they paid their fares in advance.

It is probable that not even the shrewd and wise old Dunker foresaw the many evasions of the law. The newlanders told the Germans that if they would not say "Ja! ja!" to the inspectors who asked them whether they had enough room and food during the voyage, they would be detained on board for four weeks, on account of a law suit which would follow. The fear of a longer detention on the uncomfortable vessel was often sufficient to silence the simple-minded Germans.[223] We can well imagine Saur's impotent grief when he published this item in 1752. Two years later he inquired in despair whether there were not one or two honest "Visitators" who would go on board the ships in order to see whether the terms of the contracts had been observed.[224]

From 1755 to 1764 very few Germans came to America on account of the dangers incident to the French and Indian War. In the fall of 1764 vessels with Germans began to arrive again. Miller had an advertisement in his paper of November 12 announcing the arrival of several hundred German servants who were for sale. About two months later[225] he reported that eleven ships had arrived from Rotterdam between August 8 and December 4, having two thousand three hundred and twenty-eight full fares, or (according to Miller's estimate) about three thousand people. With the reappearance of immigrants the former scenes of distress were repeated. In November, 1764, an appeal for help for the sick Germans in the hospital was published in the *Staatsbote*.[226]

[223] S 12-1-52.
[224] S 1-1-55.
[225] M 157.
[226] M 149.

At last some of the leading Germans of Philadelphia decided that the best way to ameliorate the conditions of the immigrants was to organize a society for the purpose of systematizing the work before them. On November 30, 1764, a meeting was held to organize a "Deutsche Gesellschaft."[227] The rules of the society were drawn up between this date and December 26, when a permanent organization was effected,[228] with Heinrich Keppele, a Philadelphia merchant, as president.[229] It was probably the first charitable organization among the Germans in America. The aim of the society was at least twofold; firstly to secure the enactment of more stringent laws relating to the living conditions during the sea voyage, and secondly to gather food, clothing and money for the help of the indigent immigrants on their arrival in Philadelphia. In January, 1765, it presented to the governor of the province an English translation of its constitution.[230] In 1766 the *Staatsbote* boasted that most of the immigrants were now assigned to other colonies because the Pennsylvania laws were too strict.[231] These laws had presumably been passed at the instigation of the society. That its second aim was not forgotten is amply proved by the treasurers' reports, which appeared regularly in the papers. Considerable sums of money were collected and disbursed in order to alleviate the misery of the immigrants. For example, in 1768 one township of Lancaster County sent six thou-

---

[227] M 153.
[228] M 155.
[229] Christopher Saur, the second, was not an officer or even a member of the society. Although the leading spirits were men who belonged to the denominations opposed to him, there is hardly any doubt that he gave his powerful support to the young organization.
[230] M 157.
[231] M 241.

Charities and Humanitarian Organizations. 65

sand pounds of flour and some money to the society.[232] The "Deutsche Gesellschaft" was incorporated on September 19, 1781, by an act of the Pennsylvania Assembly.[233] It broadened the scope of its activities by helping young men to obtain a college education.[234] It is still in existence at the present time, helping those that are in need of aid.

Despite all efforts, the lot of the redemptioners was often most wretched, because the laws were still not comprehensive enough. For instance, in 1767 the Germans were powerless to prevent the ship companies from raising the fare seven pounds for the immigrants, while the fare of the ordinary passengers remained unchanged. Not only was this an unjust discrimination, but it also forced the immigrants to remain on shipboard much longer because the inhabitants of the province hesitated to pay such a high price for their services.[235] This prolonged detention caused great distress, as we learn from an article in the *Staatsbote*,[236] which reported that the fifty persons not yet sold had at last been permitted to come on shore, but since the merchants in whose ship they had arrived gave them no food, they were walking through the streets with the children crying for bread. Even after somebody had paid the increased fares the privations of the immigrants did not cease, since they had to serve longer than in former times.[235]

The system of redemptioning was still in vogue after the War for Independence.[237] Although Kuhns says[238] the

[232] M 315.
[233] PC 23.
[234] See Chapter IV.
[235] M 306.
[236] M 309.
[237] See NUL 1-6, 12, 14, 109; DP 39; NUR 604.
[238] German and Swiss Settlements in Pennsylvania, p. 80.

worst cases of the abuse of the system occurred after the Revolution, the newspapers do not mention them. In fact it is highly improbable that the later cases were so shocking as those of the colonial days. It is quite certain that the abuses were less frequent during the later period.

When the Germans in America extended aid to the redemptioners and endeavored to remedy the flagrant abuses of the redemptioning system, they simply did for their relatives and countrymen what duty required. But, on occasion, they also gave their support to charitable and humanitarian enterprises, when they were not so directly concerned and when they could have easily withheld their support without creating much unfavorable comment. In 1751 an act was passed by the Pennsylvania Assembly to erect a hospital in Philadelphia for the indigent sick and insane.[239] In Saur's paper of August 16, 1751, he printed an appeal to the Germans for aid in this undertaking. The article urged that, although the Germans had to help their poor countrymen who arrived in America every year, they should also support the hospital. That this appeal was not without its effect is curiously proved by an address[240] delivered in February, 1794, before the Society for the Support of the Needy Poor in the German Evangelical Lutheran Congregation of Philadelphia. This address gives a history of charity in Philadelphia. The speaker said that Mathias Koplin, a German, gave in 1751 a piece of land lying between Germantown and Philadelphia to the hospital. He attached one condition to the gift, namely, that he would not be required to go to Philadelphia every year to vote for the twelve directors or trus-

[239] S 133.
[240] Printed in full, PC₂ 277, 278.

tees of the hospital.²⁴¹ The letter (dated September 2, 1751) which Koplin wrote to Saur on the subject was read by the speaker.

When the French and Indian War broke out, the Indian allies of the French swarmed through the mountain passes of Pennsylvania, attacked with savage ruthlessness the frontier settlers and compelled the survivors to flee to the more densely inhabited parts of the colony. Without food and shelter and often without sufficient clothing, they were indeed wretched, pitiable specimens of humanity. Those Pennsylvania Germans who were not driven from their homes helped generously in providing for the refugees. In the fall of 1755 Lancaster County was crowded with fugitives in dire want. Then the Mennonites showed the kindly spirit which animated them by collecting several wagon loads of flour, meat and clothes for the unfortunate ones.²⁴² A month later there was even greater distress in Northampton County because many settlers fled to the Moravian towns of Bethlehem and Nazareth after they had heard of the Gnadenhütten massacre.²⁴³ On learning of the condition of affairs, the Mennonites of Skippack, Montgomery County, immediately dispatched seven wagon loads of flour and other provisions to the Moravian settlements.²⁴⁴ The Lutherans, the Reformed and the Schwenkfelders also collected and sent provisions.²⁴⁵

In 1791 Germans of Philadelphia organized a "Gesellschaft," which had the following aims: to aid its sick mem-

---

[241] This is thoroughly characteristic of the Mennonites and the Dunkers, who are always willing to give liberally for humanitarian purposes but usually dislike political responsibility.

[242] S 187.

[243] See Chapter II.

[244] S 188.

[245] S 2-1-56.

bers, to give them a decent burial and to help their widows and orphans.[246] Apparently it was a forerunner of our present-day lodges. In the winter of 1791–1792 Valentin Krug, a brewer of Lancaster, had the misfortune of losing all his possessions by fire. The people of the city immediately began to collect money in order to aid him in rebuilding his house and brewery.[247]

The Germans helped to alleviate the misery caused by the terrible yellow fever epidemics of 1793, 1797, 1798 and 1799 in Philadelphia. When almost all able-bodied persons, both rich and poor, were fleeing from the plague-stricken city in 1793, Johann Kühmle, an influential German druggist, remained to tend the sick,[248] risking his life as Stephen Girard did in the same outbreak of the scourge. He treated several hundred patients in the six or eight weeks during which the fever was at its worst.[249] In 1797 the people of Lancaster city and county sent to the poor of Philadelphia more than one thousand dollars in money and three hundred and seventy barrels and two hundred and twenty-three pounds of flour.[250] Again in 1798 it was announced that the people of Lancaster were aiding the fever-stricken mothers of Philadelphia.[251]

The various religious denominations undoubtedly provided for their poor, although the newspapers mentioned this form of charity very rarely. However, such aid was probably the most important and the most widespread, even if the least ostentatious. We find[252] that the Luth-

---
[246] PC₃ 53.
[247] NUR 154.
[248] PC₂ 254.
[249] PC₂ 256.
[250] DP 2.
[251] DP 42.
[252] PC₃ 277, 278.

eran congregation of Philadelphia held special collections prior to 1784 for its poor. Beginning with that year it set aside for the poor the collections of its evening prayer meetings after having deducted the cost of light. On February 1, 1790, the congregation organized "Die Gesellschaft zur Unterstützung der Hülfsbedürftigen Armen in der Deutsch Evangelisch Lutherischen Gemeinde." In four years the membership of this society had increased from fourteen to almost two hundred. In 1791 the German Reformed congregation of Philadelphia started a similar society. In the winter of 1791–1792[253] the Lutherans bought fifty cords of wood to give to the poor and also helped the needy with money and bread.[254]

The German publishers were unanimously opposed to slavery. In 1760 the second Saur expressed the belief that it would have been conducive to the welfare of Pennsylvania if the importation of slaves had been forbidden at the time when the province was settled.[255] Almost a year later[256] he published a strong attack on the slave trade. The article opened by saying that Germans in America were beginning to buy slaves because they could not procure German redemptioners. Although they gave various reasons why they purchased slaves, none of the reasons would stand the test of the Golden Rule. In reality their greed was the only cause for the purchases. Up to that time Pennsylvania had been unprofitable territory for the slave dealers, because the Germans had opposed the traffic, but since some of them were now encouraging it, there was a rumor that three ships had departed for Africa.

[253] GZ₂ 86.
[254] This was not done by the above mentioned society.
[255] S 3-28-60.
[256] S 250.

Presumably the manufacturers were the most frequent purchasers of slaves. They certainly inserted the largest number of advertisements in the papers about runaway slaves. Thus Georg Adam Weidner, of Berks County, who owned a brick kiln, offered rewards for runaway slaves in 1761[257] and in 1763,[258] and Henrich Wilhelm Stiegel, the owner of an iron foundry at Mannheim, Lancaster County, informed the public in 1763 that one of his[259] slaves had run away. Saur published Weidner's advertisement of 1761 in his paper. He appended, however, an editorial note in which he said he was amazed that the negro ran away barefooted and with poor clothes. If the masters had been doing what was right, many of the slaves would not have thought of running away; but greed is the root of all evil.

Toward the close of the century the protests against slavery became very common. In 1787 the *Neue Unpartheyische Lancäster Zeitung* published in installments the story of Walter Mifflin, a Quaker who had freed his slaves.[260] It was printed for the purpose of helping the anti-slavery cause. In 1788, one hundred years after the first protest against slavery by the German Quakers of Germantown, the Lutheran synod went on record against slavery.[261] Reiche in his "General Postbothe" told his readers that Congress could not abolish slavery, because such an act would give Congress the power to confiscate all property. Like original sin, we could not get rid of slav-

---

[257] S 7-3-61.
[258] M 94.
[259] M 94.
[260] NUL 7, 15, 16, 17.
[261] NUL 46.

ery entirely, but we should eliminate it as nearly as possible.[262]

In 1794 the following poem, with the title "Lied eines Negersclaven in America," was reprinted from the *Göttinger Musenalmanach*[263] of 1784 by the *Philadelphische Correspondenz*:[264]

1. Hinter'm Meeres-Strande,
Wo die Sonn' erwacht;
Fern, aus jenem Lande,
Bin ich hergebracht.

2. Raja, mein Gebieter,
Gab, um Feuertrank,
Einem weissen Wüter,
Mich auf Lebenslang,

3. Bin ein Mensch, wie Weisse,
Habe nichts gethan;
Plagen mich mit Fleisse,
Sehn als Thier mich an.

4. Lasten zum Erdrücken
Sind mir aufgelegt,
Blut färbt meinen Rücken,
Wenn die Geissel schlägt.

5. Nicht um sie zu ätzen
Duld' ich alle Pein;
Steine, die sie schätzen,
Tauschen sie drum ein.

6. Und heim lebt' ich friedlich!
Gegen jeden mild,
Theilt' ich gern und gütlich,
Was mein Pfeil erzielt.

7. Weib von Dir gerissen,
Dir geraubt bin ich!
Muszt den Gatten missen,
Härmst dich ab um mich.

[262] GP 27.
[263] Göttinger Musenalmanach, 1784, p. 88.
[264] PC₁ 269.

8. Ach! und meiner Kleinen,
Meiner Kinder Noth!
    Jammern jetzt und weinen,
Sind vielleicht schon todt.

9. Weisz, ihr fleht zu Gotte,
Dasz er günstig sey,
    Thut ihr's nicht zum Spotte?
Weisse! gebt mich frey.

This poem thoroughly expresses not only the sympathy which the Pennsylvania German felt toward the slaves, but also the moral indignation aroused in him by the slave horror.

CHAPTER IV.

THE EDUCATION AND THE EDUCATIONAL FACILITIES OF THE PENNSYLVANIA GERMANS.

A. Schools.[265]

THE educational problem facing the German Americans of the eighteenth century was a difficult one. Since most of the immigrants belonged to the peasant class, they usually had a very poor education, if any at all. The number of illiterates was undoubtedly very large. In 1754 an article was published in London describing the condition of affairs in the province of Pennsylvania.[266] To the author's assertion that one half of the Germans were uneducated ("ungelehrsam!"), Saur replied[267] that he doubted the accuracy of this statement. ("Hieran ist sehr zu zweifeln.") However, he did not deny that the num-

---

[265] This chapter does not presume to give a complete history of German American education in the eighteenth century. I have limited myself almost entirely to material which I found in the Pennsylvania German newspapers. It is well known that some schools were established before 1750 by the various denominations. Not only the Lutherans and the Reformed but also the Moravians and the Dunkers started elementary schools. For a brief account of the schools before 1760, see S. E. Weber's "The Charity School Movement in Colonial Pennsylvania."

[266] Probably by the Reverend William Smith, although Saur thought the Reverend Mr. Schlatter was the author.

[267] S 184.

ber of uneducated persons was quite large. Probably the percentage of illiteracy was higher in the middle of the century than at any other time. The life of a pioneer was usually too arduous to allow him to think of giving his children even a rudimentary education. In addition to this, even if he desired to do so the facilities were lacking, since there were often neither schoolhouses nor teachers. Consequently the first generation of the descendants of the immigrants were more uneducated than the immigrants themselves.

I. ELEMENTARY SCHOOLS.

1. *Before 1780.*

By 1750, however, many of the Germans had successfully passed through the early vicissitudes of a pioneer life and were beginning to turn their attention to the education of their children. Lotteries were organized to raise money for the erection of schoolhouses. For instance, a lottery was started to pay for the schoolhouse and for the parsonage of the Lutheran congregation in Germantown;[268] another one was begun for the purpose of raising money to build a schoolhouse for the German Reformed congregation of Philadelphia;[268] the Lutherans in Reading started a lottery in 1755 so that they might obtain funds to purchase a school building.[269] In these first years of the second half of the century we also find an increasing number of teachers among the immigrants. According to Saur's paper of June 1, 1750, a German teacher was confined in the Philadelphia prison because he did not have sufficient money to pay for his passage. Again in 1753 a teacher and his wife offered themselves as indentured ser-

[268] S 160.
[269] S 11–1–55.

vants for three and a half years in order to pay the expenses of the voyage.[270]

A society was formed in England in 1753 for the purpose of establishing so-called free or charity schools among the Pennsylvania Germans, in which both the English and German languages should be taught without charge. The Lutherans and the Reformed gladly accepted the offer, the Reverend Mr. Schlatter of the Reformed church being appointed superintendent of the schools. However, the sectarians, led by Saur, attacked the schools on the ground that they were organized for the purpose of making the Germans forget their own language. They bitterly resented the imputation that they might become disloyal to the colony if they preserved their native tongue.[271] Saur asked why the Irish, the Swedes and the Welsh were allowed to retain their language, while the Germans were expected to speak English.[272] Saur's question forms a part of the comment on the news item that six English free schools for Germans were to be opened by an English society and would be located at Philadelphia, Lancaster, Yorcktaun, Reading, Easton, etc.

How long the charity schools remained in existence is not known. Saur's paper does not mention them after 1756, although some were still in existence in 1763.[273] The references to them in 1756 show that influences were at work which would cause their failure. Saur reported that Schlatter was not popular among the Germans of Pennsylvania because of his favorable attitude toward the

[270] S 159.
[271] For a history of the struggle for the preservation of their language, see Chapter V.
[272] S 9-1-54.
[273] Weber, op. cit., p. 55.

free schools.²⁷⁴ In another issue he announced that Johann Wilhelm Wiegand, the teacher of the free school in Philadelphia, who had been teaching sixty children for one year, had received only five pounds of his salary from the treasurer.²⁷⁵ The schools were unsuccessful probably for two reasons. They apparently did not have sufficient financial backing; and, again, many Germans, always alarmed at any attempt to anglicize them, refused to patronize the schools after Saur had called their attention to the danger. However, these schools produced one good result. They caused the various denominations to make more determined efforts to provide adequate educational facilities for the young.

The Lutheran and the Reformed congregations in the rural districts began to insert advertisements for teachers in the Philadelphia papers. The first of these advertisements which I have discovered is found in Saur's paper of May 16, 1756. It says that a teacher is wanted in "Emety Taunschip" (Berks County). The advertisements increased in frequency up to about 1770. Between 1770 and 1775 the teachers inserted more advertisements, offering their services.²⁷⁶ This seems to indicate that the supply now exceeded the demand. After the outbreak of the war the schools had difficulty in obtaining teachers. On January 5, 1776, the German Reformed congregation of Philadelphia advertised for a teacher.²⁷⁷ In 1779 the Germantown Union School had no English and no German teacher. The successful applicants for the positions were each promised a house, garden and orchard without rent.²⁷⁸

[274] S 7-1-56.
[275] S 5-1-56.
[276] M 618 et al.
[277] M 761.
[278] M 919.

It is rather difficult to determine what the teachers were ordinarily required to teach in these schools because the advertisements usually did not specify this. Undoubtedly they taught reading, writing and arithmetic. It is safe to assume that they also gave catechetical instruction, for there is abundant evidence[279] that they did so in the period following the war. They were probably also the church organists. For instance, in advertising for a teacher the German Reformed congregation of Philadelphia[277] required that the candidate should know how to play the organ. Girls received instruction in sewing in the Germantown Union School.[280]

In Philadelphia, German evening schools were started at least as early as 1754. In this year Johann Wolfgang Leitzel, "deutscher Schul-und Rechen Meister" at the lower end of Germantown, advertised that he was conducting a night school, both in summer and in winter.[281] The subjects were writing and ciphering. In 1763 Johann Michael Enderlein opened a German school in Philadelphia. The hours were from six to eight, from eight to twelve in the morning, from two to five in the afternoon and from six to nine in the evening.[282] He was willing to teach reading, spelling and ciphering in English and in German. In 1774 we find an advertisement[283] announcing that a German day and night school would be started in the Northern Liberties of Philadelphia; the subjects taught would be reading, Christianity, German and English writing, cipher-

---

[279] See below.
[280] M 919.
[281] S 170.
[282] M 80.
[283] M 665.

ing, history, geography, letter writing, public speaking, science, and, if desired, French.[284]

2. Elementary Schools; After 1780.

(a) *In the Rural Districts.*—After the war the various papers contained many advertisements for rural district teachers. Since the schools were increasing rapidly in number, the supply of teachers was entirely inadequate. In 1798 the statement was made that the teaching force in country districts was very incompetent because teachers with hardly any qualifications were permitted to give instruction. Very few capable men wanted to teach because the salary of country teachers was disproportionately small in comparison with the income of other people.[285] Part of the teacher's salary often consisted in the free use of a house and garden. For instance, the Reformed congregation of Bern, Berks County, offered to the teacher a good garden and meadow,[286] and the Lutheran teacher at Tulpehocken was promised thirty-five acres of land, a two-story house, a barn and enough meadow land for four head of cattle.[287]

In most of these country schools the instruction was entirely in German, although both English and German were taught in some of them. The subjects were usually reading, writing and arithmetic. Moreover, the teacher, as stated above, was ordinarily required to act as organist in the church[288] and to give catechetical instruction.[289] It is

---

[284] I do not know whether the three last mentioned schools belonged to religious denominations, but probably not.
[285] DP 19.
[286] PC 120.
[287] A 135. This was undoubtedly an unusually liberal offer.
[288] PC 120, 166; PC₂ 334; NUR 299 et al.
[289] NUR 592 et al.

difficult to determine what kind of pedagogical methods the schoolmasters employed. The only reference I have found to methods was contained in a letter written by a Berks County to a Lancaster County teacher, in which the writer attacked the new method of teaching the children to read before they could spell.[290]

The religious denominations were desirous of retaining elementary education within their control. When Doctor Logan in 1800 proposed to the Pennsylvania Assembly a State school system by means of which the schools would become secularized, many German papers attacked the plan. The *Neue Unpartheyische Readinger Zeitung* opposed it for three reasons:[291] the congregations would have no voice in selecting or dismissing teachers; the teachers would not be required to give catechetical instruction; everybody, no matter whether he had children or not, would have to pay taxes for the support of the schools. The York *Volksberichter*, edited by the Reverend Mr. Görring, was also reported[292] to have attacked the proposed school system on the ground that parents would have no opportunity to give a religious education to their children; if the people would be compelled to support non-denominational schools, it would be not only an infringement on their religious freedom, but also a burden. Although the Reading *Adler* supported Doctor Logan,[293] his bill never passed, presumably on account of German opposition.

Because many of the rural Pennsylvania Germans were

[290] NUL, 54. Attention should be called to the rules of Christopher Dock, which are printed in Saur's Geistliches Magazien. Dock was a teacher of the sectarians and lived about the middle of the eighteenth century.

[291] NUR 592.

[292] NUR 602.

[293] A 208.

unable to speak English, they were accused of being illiterate. This accusation was definitely refuted by the German papers. In 1790 the *Philadelphische Correspondenz* stated that in most townships of Pennsylvania there were less than four natives who could neither read nor write.[294] In 1800 the statement was made that schoolhouses were connected with almost all churches.[295] The rural Pennsylvania Germans were determined that their descendants should have at least an elementary education. We find that a new school in New Holland, Lancaster County, was in charge of thirteen trustees in 1786.[296] The subscribers to the school, out of their own number, elected them for a term of three years. The trustees who resigned had to pay a fine of twenty shillings, and those who absented themselves from the semi-annual meetings without good cause were fined five shillings.

However, despite these determined efforts to improve educational facilities in the country districts, conditions were far from satisfactory. The children of the very poor could not attend the schools because they were unable to pay the cost of tuition. Some hired out their children to other people on condition that the children be given schooling and catechetical instruction.[297] The education of a great many children was exceedingly slight. The *Readinger Zeitung*[298] gave the following reasons for this: some parents did not send their children to school until they were sixteen years of age, while others sent them very irregularly; some did not send them at all on account of

[294] PC, 14.
[295] NUR 592.
[296] PC 287.
[297] NUR 592.
[298] NUR 510, 511, 512.

miserliness or for fear that the children would be punished in school; others attempted to give them instruction at home with very unsatisfactory results. The English and the Irish, the paper continued, put the Germans to shame in this respect, since they began to send their children to school as soon as they could carry books, and were not satisfied until their offspring had thoroughly learned reading, writing and arithmetic.[209] Thus did the press attempt to stir the German people to emulation.

(b) *In the Larger Towns.*—In the towns educational facilities for the Germans were much more satisfactory. Most of the towns like Reading,[300] Lancaster and Philadelphia[300] had elementary denominational schools, which had been in existence for forty or fifty years. A Lutheran school was established in Lancaster before 1750—a statement which is proved by the obituary notice[301] of Jacob Löser, who died on January 3, 1793, after having taught in the Lutheran school of Lancaster for forty-four years. In 1782 Lancaster had several German schools.[302]

Unquestionably Philadelphia led the State in elementary education for the Germans. The Lutherans not only conducted their regular denominational pay schools, but also organized in 1786 a free school for the poor children of the denomination.[303] The congregation paid the teacher of this school and provided the children with books, paper, etc. In 1792 eighty pupils were in attendance at the free school,[304] and by 1794 several hundred had received instruction there.[303]

[209] This statement is probably an exaggeration for the purpose of spurring the Germans to more vigorous action.
[300] See above.
[301] NUL 285.
[302] PC 62.
[303] PC₂ 277, 278.
[304] GZ₂ 86.

Fortunately we have a fairly good picture of the Lutheran elementary schools of Philadelphia in 1796. In that year a series of articles by "Philoteutologos" appeared in the *Philadelphische Correspondenz* on the Lutheran schools of Philadelphia.[305] The author indicated in the first article the external defects of the schools.[306] Although no teacher should have had more than fifty or sixty pupils, one German teacher in Philadelphia instructed almost one hundred, two others more than seventy each; and it was reported that still another had more than one hundred and thirty.[307] The tuition for each pupil was eleven shillings a quarter, while the pupils in the English schools paid eighteen, twenty, thirty and thirty-five shillings a quarter. The tuition was paid directly to the teachers of the German schools by the parents, so that the salaries varied according to the number in attendance. The pupils sat so close together that there was always opportunity for the mischievous ones to torment the others. "Philoteutologos" also expressed the fear that many children attended the free school when their parents could afford to send them to the other schools.

In the second article[308] he discussed the internal defects of the school, as he called them. After having attended a school for five or six years, the pupils could read and write, but their learning was like that of parrots. The only text-books were the Bible, the catechism and the A B C book. "Philoteutologos" criticized the Bible as

---

[305] PC_2 485, 487, 488, 490, 491, 493, 497. (No. 485 is found in the Harvard Library and the others in the State Library of Pennsylvania, although 493 is also found in PHS.)

[306] PC_2 485.

[307] Some of these schools were probably under the control of other denominations. See below.

[308] PC_2 487, 488.

a text-book because it was not graded. There was too much parrot-like memorizing, singing and praying in the schools, and the curriculum consisted only of religion, German reading, writing and arithmetic. In the opinion of the writer some English should have been taught.

The other articles gave the constructive criticism of "Philoteutologos." He desired that there should be only one class of schools for rich and poor and no "poor" schools. He suggested the following curriculum: the English and German Languages; the fundamentals of religion; ciphering in English, together with a little geometry, trigonometry and algebra; geography; history of Germany, America, Rome and Greece.[309] He would have divided the school into seven classes as follows: first class, German letters, syllables and words; second class, reading an easy German book, writing; third class, continuation of reading and writing, study of catechism, German grammar[310] and English, reading and interpreting the New Testament on Friday; fourth class, continuation of the work of the third class and, in addition, English grammar and writing; fifth class, continuation of the work of the fourth class, reading best prose and poetic works, Old Testament on Friday, ciphering; sixth class, continuation of the work of the fifth class; seventh class, higher mathematics, composition, geography, history, natural science and ethics.[311] There were to be four teachers, two for the German subjects of the first six classes, one for the English subjects of these classes and one for the seventh class who knew both languages.[311] The writer also urged the value of public

[309] PC₂ 490.

[310] He wanted somebody to write a German grammar for use in the schools.

[311] PC₂ 491.

examinations.[312] He gave a detailed account of the tuition which was to be charged and a description of the schoolhouse to be erected. He insisted that the sexes should be separated.[313]

While these articles emphasized the defects of the existing schools, the fact that a leading German paper devoted so much space to both destructive and constructive criticism indicated that the Germans of Philadelphia were thoroughly alive to the necessity of giving their children an elementary education. "Philoteutologos" said[314] that one hundred and eighty pupils were enrolled in 1796 in the Lutheran schools of Philadelphia alone; in addition, many children of German extraction were attending the English schools because the German schools offered them no opportunity to study English.

The leading Germans in general desired their brethren to have sufficient education to enable them to display a more intelligent interest in local and national affairs. This desire was often expressed in the newspapers.[315] On January 9, 1788, the following eloquent paragraph appeared in the *Neue Unpartheyische Lancäster Zeitung:*

> Möchte doch jede kleine Landstadt, die in Verbindung mit der umliegenden Gegend 3, 4 Wirthshäuser zu Verderben der Jugend im Flor erhalten kan, sich durch ähnliche Anstalten (i.e., elementary schools) auszeichnen! Möchten unsere lieben Deutschen sich einmal überzeugen dasz Schulen leiblichen und geistlichen Segen mit sich führen, dasz sie uns Bürgerliche-und Gewissensfreyheit sichern, dasz sie uns zu einer erleuchteten Nation erheben, dasz sie unsern Kindern und Kindeskindern das unschätzbare, mit

---

[312] PC₂ 493.
[313] PC₂ 497.
[314] PC₂ 491.
[315] See NUR 1, 510; NUL 55–58 et al.

so vielem Blute erkaufte Gut, erst recht geniessen lassen, freye Bürger in Amerika zu seyn.

There was little danger that the Pennsylvania Germans would become uneducated and unintelligent citizens when their leaders saw so clearly the need of an education.[316]

The Moravians of Bethlehem were conducting in 1787 a school for young girls which placed much emphasis on the finer arts. A twelve-year-old girl wrote a letter, dated August 16, 1787, to her brother in a school in Connecticut.[317] She said that about thirty girls of her age were rooming in the same building where she was. Every morning they rose at six o'clock and, after washing and combing, went for worship into a little chapel which was attached to the school. Their morning and evening services consisted of religious hymns, which they accompanied on their zithers. No man was permitted to come into the chapel. At seven they had breakfast and at eight school commenced. They studied English and German[318] reading and grammar, writing, ciphering, history, geography, composition, etc., up to eleven o'clock. Then they went to chapel, where a man gave them a short religious and moral talk, and the organist played on a large organ. At a quarter of twelve dinner was served. In the afternoon they were taught sewing, embroidering, painting and music. School was dismissed at three o'clock and supper was served at six. At half past seven evening worship began, and at eight they retired into a large room, where all of them slept. On Sunday they attended religious services in a large chapel, where the whole school assembled. The

---
[316] See Chapter VIII.
[317] PC 371.
[318] Only one language was required, but both could be studied if desired.

sermons were sometimes in German and sometimes in English. The singing was very pretty and was accompanied by violins, bass viols and organs. There were two women teachers in the school in addition to the one who taught music, and one male teacher, who gave instruction in grammar. The young girl added that there was an academy for boys at Nazareth corresponding to the girls' school.

II. HIGHER INSTITUTIONS OF LEARNING.

While the German religious denominations were unanimous in their approval of elementary instruction, some of them were aggressively opposed to higher education. The reasons for this opposition were well and emphatically stated by Saur. When the University of Pennsylvania was established he inserted the following in his paper:[319]

Die Vorschläge und Einrichtung zu einer Hohen Schule ist gedruckt, und stellet vor, dasz darinen gelehret werden solle, Lateinisch, Griechisch, Frantzösisch, Spanisch, Teutsch und Englisch nach dem Grund der Sprach. Auch soll die Jugend unterweissen werden im Schreiben, Rechnen, in Historien von alten Geschichten und die beschreibung des Erdbodens, in der Meszkunst, der Wohlredenheit, natürlichen Philosophia, und was verschiedenen Handwercksleuten dienen kan, um Abrisse zu machen, und noch in anderen verschiedenen Dingen wovon Salomon sagt: Gott habe den menschen aufrichtig gemacht; aber sie suchen viel Künste, die theils zum natürlichen Leben dienen, theils dem wahren Christen thun mehr hinderlich als nützlich sind; dan die edle Zeit da sie solten trachten am ersten nach dem Reich Gottes und nach seiner Gerechtigkeit wird verschwendet mit Sachen durch welche dem menschen zum Stoltz, Hochmütig und reich zu werden Gelegenheit gegeben wird, wovon Christus sagt: Wie schwerlich werden die Reichen ins Reich Gottes kommen;

[319] S 118 (March 16, 1750).

es ist leichter etc. Und Paulus fragt; Wo sind die Klugen? Wo sind die Weltweissen? Hat nicht Gott dieser Welt Weisheit zur Thorheit gemacht? Im Plan ist nichts gemeldet vom Prediger Machen, von Layer und Doctor Machen, dan es folgt hernach; Die ersten beyden brauchen nur ein gutes Mundstück, um ihr Gedächtnusz auszuleeren. Und der letzten sind schon mehr als gut ist: Viele machen sich selbst, durch anderer Leute Schaden, oder verlust des Lebens.

In the next number of his paper Saur elaborated his attacks upon colleges. He said he was not opposed to a good education for the young people, as a writer in the *Philadelphia Fama* claimed. Saur granted that college students learned everything necessary for their temporal welfare. If a student wished to become great, rich, esteemed and honored, to have easy times in life, to rule over his fellowmen, that wish came from Lucifer. If the desire to dance and fight was added to it, nothing appeared to such students more despicable than a Christian life.

Hat einer auf Hohen Schulen neben Philosophi (viel losze Vieh) auch die Natur aller Kräuter, Wurtzeln, Thiere, Metallen und alles was mineralisch ist kennen lernen, verstehet auch den gantzen menschlichen Cörper zu anatomieren, und denckt er kenne und wisse alle Gebrechen des menschlichen Leibes nach dem besten Unterricht, den die erfahreneste und geübte Meister auf den Schulen geben können, und bekehret sich hernach zu Gott, von gantzem Hertzen, und sein Verstand wird mit Göttlichem Licht erleuchtet, so wird er in Verwunderung zum Preisz Gottes sagen: Dieser Welt Weiszheit ist doch nur Thorheit bey Gott!

He then used the lives of Christ and Paul as illustrations and promised to publish in the future what Luther said of colleges for the benefit of those who did not believe Christ and Paul.

In 1754 Saur thought that the English society, organized for the purpose of establishing free schools[320] among the Germans, was planning to start a college for Germans. This mistake occasioned the following attack:[321]

> Wir hören, dasz der Ehrgeitz, Geldgeitz und Wollust eine Anstalt gemacht, dasz zu Philadelphia eine Hohe Schule aufgerichtet werden, vor die Teutschen die nicht arbeiten mögen, oder eine ehrliche Hanthierung treiben; vermuthlich unterm Vorwand dasz man Advocaten, Doctor und Prediger hier im Lande selber machen könne, weil so wenig Gutes herein komt.

About forty years later Saur's grandson, Samuel Saur, also published an attack on higher education in his paper, *Die Chesnuthiller Wochenschrift*.[322] He quoted Luther as saying that it would be much better if all colleges were burned to powder, for nothing more hellish or devilish has ever been erected than these.[323] Saur asserted that educated men were not steadfast, the colleges were the assembling places of rascals, and that hardly anything was taught in them except disputation. Atheistical and deistical books were written by college men. Students in higher institutions of learning learned to write novels, tragedies and comedies, the purpose of which was to entertain vain people. Even Gellert once wrote a comedy, although later he was sorry that he had done it.

Although the influential Saurs maintained such a determined opposition to higher education, we must not lose sight of the fact that the leaders, both secular and religious, of the Lutherans, the Reformed and the Moravians were unanimously in favor of it. We have seen that Böhm's

---

[320] See above.
[321] S 169.
[322] CW 99. 102, 104.
[323] Luther did not condemn all higher and secondary education, as is well known.

Fama disagreed[324] with Saur's attitude in 1750, and that the Lutheran and the Reformed ministers were often instructors at the various colleges.[325] Henrich Miller published in 1771 a long account of the commencement exercises of the academy which later became the University of Pennsylvania.[326] He was particularly pleased that four medical students graduated in that year. When he heard the report in 1769 that an academy was to be established at Reading, he said that such a school at that place would undoubtedly confer great benefits upon the inhabitants, and especially upon the youth of the province, and would be an eternal glory to its founders and supporters.[327]

A German seminary was founded in Philadelphia in 1773. Its purpose was threefold: to help the English youths to study German, to aid the German youths to obtain some useful knowledge, no matter what occupation they intended to follow in later life, and to give the German American youths a good foundation in order that they might later enjoy so much the more advantageously the benefits of the English academies in Philadelphia and elsewhere.[328] That the school was entirely under the supervision of the Lutheran congregation of Philadelphia is proved by the request that all subscriptions for the school be given to the Lutheran ministers or to certain private individuals and by the fact that all prospective students had to report to the ministers of this congregation.[329] The seminary was probably never very flourishing. On June

[324] See above.
[325] See Chapter II and also below.
[326] M 495.
[327] M 393.
[328] M 645.
[329] M 597.

29, 1773, only fourteen students were enrolled, although five more were expected. In 1774 the teaching corps of the school consisted of the Lutheran ministers with John Gartley, the English teacher, and Daniel Lehman, a young man twenty years old, who had received his education at Strassburg.[330] In the same year a lottery was organized,[331] the proceeds of which were to be given to the seminary. The institution probably came to an end when the British seized Philadelphia in the fall of 1777. At any rate, the last reference to it in the newspapers is found in the *Staatsbote* of September 3, 1777.

In 1780 the University of Pennsylvania started a German institute or academy in connection with its preparatory department. The Reverend Mr. Kunze, the Lutheran minister, had charge of it at first; after his removal to New York, his colleague, the Reverend Mr. Helmuth, succeeded him.[332] The first notice of this school found in the German papers is in the *Philadelphische Correspondenz* of April 10, 1782, when the report was made that four young German Americans had been admitted into the university from the German Academy. The trustees of the university intended to place a teacher of English in the academy, and the professor of German at the former would also be tutor in the latter. It was further announced that they would withdraw this offer unless a minimum of thirty students would take advantage of it. The *Deutsche Gesellschaft* of Philadelphia promised to pay for two of these students.[333] At the university's commencement in 1784 one German, Heinrich Stuber, received his baccalaureate

---

[330] M 645.
[331] M 656. The proceeds were to be 1012 pounds 10 shillings.
[332] See Dubbs's "History of Franklin and Marshall College," pp. 8–9.
[333] See Chapter III.

degree. He had begun to study when the German Department was organized four years before.[334] On September 20, 1784, the German students of the institute showed their proficiency before the assembled members of the *Deutsche Gesellschaft* by rendering a varied program.[335] In 1785 seventy Germans were attending the institute. They studied English and German reading and writing, Latin, Greek, mathematics, history and geography, with French as an elective; particular attention was given to public speaking. The tuition was six pounds a year.[336]

This institute, however, did not satisfy the ambition of the German leaders, who desired a German college in Pennsylvania. They felt that such an institution would attract students of all religious denominations, while the academy in Philadelphia would probably be considered a Lutheran school because the ministers of that denomination were on the instructing staff. They probably also thought that many Germans were deterred from entering an English college because they would be derided by the students of English descent. As early as August 9, 1785, an article appeared in the *Philadelphische Correspondenz* which urged the establishment of a German college. One month later the same paper published a long article on the advisability of starting a non-denominational German college. The writer expressed the opinion that such a school was necessary in order that the Germans might be able to take an active part in public affairs; in a German college the

[334] PC 163.
[335] PC 179, 182, 183, 184.
[336] PC 227. Philip Pauli, the French and Latin teacher, offered board at thirty pounds per year. The Institute was still in existence in 1789. On July 30 of that year Pauli delivered his farewell address and made an eloquent plea that the Germans should take advantage of the opportunity offered by the University, and by the Deutsche Gesellschaft. (See PC 435.)

Germans would not be discouraged by being termed "Dutchman" and "Sour Crout," as happened in the English colleges. He suggested that Lancaster would be a good place for the school because the city was centrally located.[337]

On December 11, 1786, a petition for a charter for Franklin College at Lancaster was presented to the Pennsylvania Assembly. The college was to have forty trustees, of whom fourteen were to be Lutheran, fourteen Reformed and the remainder chosen from members of any Christian faith.[338] The full text of the charter was printed in Steiner's paper of January 16, 1787. On Tuesday, June 5, 1787, the trustees chose[339] the following officers and instructors: Principal, the Reverend Heinrich Mühlenberg;[340] Vice Principal, the Reverend Wilhelm Händel;[341] professor of Latin, Greek, and German, the Reverend Friedrich Valentin Melsheimer;[342] professor of mathemathics, William Reichenbach; professor of the English language and fine arts, the Reverend Joseph Hutchins.[343] On the next day the dedication exercises were held in the German Lutheran church of Lancaster.[344] Before the exercises the leading citizens of the town went in procession from the courthouse to the church. In this procession were found the faculty and trustees of the college, the members of the Reformed Coetus and of the Lutheran Ministerium, the officers of the religious bodies of the town

[337] PC 228.
[338] PC 295; GZ 50.
[339] PC 321; GZ 63.
[340] Lutheran.
[341] Reformed.
[342] Lutheran.
[343] Episcopal.
[344] PC 321; GZ 63.

and various other prominent men. The Reformed, Lutheran, Episcopalian and Moravian ministers took part in the dedication exercises.

At the beginning of 1788 one hundred and five students were in attendance at the new college.[345] The work done seems to have been satisfactory. In a long account of the annual examination, held on October 17, 1788, the writer expressed his particular pleasure in the fact that the students of German descent spoke English as well as those of English parentage.[346] In 1789 we are told that the students were examined, in addition to other subjects, in the Greek New Testament, Lucian and a small Greek chrestomathy, but that they made a poorer showing in Greek than in the other subjects.[347]

Although the college received some State aid in 1788[348] and received encouragement from all the German papers, it was often in financial straits. In the winter of 1788–1789 the Reverend Mr. Melsheimer wrote[349] a letter declaring that the college faced a deficit of two hundred pounds because the charges for tuition were too low. When somebody blamed this deficit on poor business management and suggested that the teachers' salaries should be reduced from two hundred to one hundred pounds a year, the answer was promptly made that the teachers had already done this of their own volition.[350] Again in 1789 the fear was expressed that the college would have to close on account of lack of funds.[351]

[345] NUL 30; PC 356.
[346] NUL 66.
[347] NUL 102.
[348] NUL 37.
[349] NUL 30; PC 356.
[350] NUL 34.
[351] NUL 102.

Probably the chief reason for these troubles was the passive, if not active, hostility of many of the Germans, particularly the sectarians. In a communication to the *Lancàster Zeitung*, "Stoffel Ehrlich," of Canostoga Township,[352] said he was opposed to the college because it would only make children wiser than their parents. He wanted his son to learn a trade. His daughter could read, but not write; she could, however, spin and cook, and was a good housekeeper. His father had not been able to read or write and yet he had been prosperous. Whether this communication expressed the views of its author or was simply a bitter satire, there is no doubt that it was a true reflection of the views of a large number of Germans. "Hannickel Wahrheit" stated in another communication[353] that the Germans often said, "Wie gelehrter wie verkehrter" and "Wer will endlich das Land bauen, wann alles gut gelernt wäre." It is consequently not surprising that many Germans with such views refused to support the college. However, Franklin College survived all vicissitudes and is now, as Franklin and Marshall College, one of the best small colleges in Pennsylvania.

Two lesser attempts to organize German secondary schools remain to be mentioned. From an advertisement[354] in May, 1793, we learn that the Reverend Friedrich Hermann intended to start a Latin school in the Germantown schoolhouse on June 17, 1793. About one year later[355] the announcement was made that on July 1, 1794, Friederich Hermann, of Germany; J. M. Ray, of Edinburgh and Paris, and others would open the Germantown

[352] NUL 2.
[353] NUL 7.
[354] PC₂ 214.
[355] PC₂ 310.

college. The following subjects would be taught: German, English, French, Latin, Greek, Oriental languages, including Hebrew and others, the philosophical sciences, "so wie alle andere Zweige gewöhnlicher und feiner Erziehung, nach einem verbesserten Plan, auf das (sic) kürzeste und practischte Art." I do not know how long the college remained in existence or even whether it was ever started. The same statement is true of another proposed educational venture, the German Catholic academy which was to be opened in Philadelphia on December 1, 1796.[356] The subjects to be taught were: penmanship (schön Schreibkunst), spelling, geography, natural sciences, letter writing and composition, general history, Latin, Italian, French, instrumental and vocal music, and ethics (moralische Vorlesungen zur Bildung des Herzens und Aufklärung des Verstandes und dergleichen).

In addition to the institutions discussed above, there were a considerable number of elementary schools and Latin schools conducted by private individuals.

B. OTHER EDUCATIONAL FACILITIES.

Besides the educational opportunities offered by schools and newspapers, the Pennsylvania Germans had their books and libraries. Some German books were published in this country during the eighteenth century and many more were imported from Germany. As may be expected, the great majority of the books read were of a religious, moral or practical nature, although some literary works were imported. Since it is not the purpose of this monograph to give a bibliography of German books printed in America, and since fairly complete bibliographies have been pub-

[356] PC$_2$ 563.

lished,[357] I shall call attention to only a few of the most important publications which are mentioned in the newspapers.

Naturally the famous Saur German Bible of 1743 deserves first mention. It is impossible to decide when Christoph Saur first conceived the idea of printing the Bible, for I have been able to find only two copies of his newspaper published prior to April 16, 1743. The issue of February 16, 1742, announces that Saur wanted to print the Bible that year, but that he would probably have to postpone the venture because he had received only a few subscriptions, although he might print enough for the subscribers and no more. Presumably, however, he did not print any before 1743. When he announced on August 16, 1743, that the unbound copies of the German Bible were ready for distribution at twelve shillings apiece, the inhabitants of America saw for the first time the entire Bible printed in a European language in the New World. Copies were later bound in sheep skin, calf skin or other leather.[358] It is to be noted that Saur said the poor could have these Bibles free of cost.[359] Although the total edition amounted to but twelve hundred copies, only one fourth of them had been sold in 1745.[360] In that year Saur also printed[361] separately the New Testament in German.[362]

Before 1760 the Lutherans, the Reformed, the Mora-

---

[357] Seidensticker's "First Century of German Printing in America"; Hildeburn's "The Issue of the Press of Pennsylvania, 1685-1784"; Bausman's "A Bibliography of Lancaster County Imprints."

[358] S 37.

[359] S 35.

[360] S 66.

[361] S 61.

[362] The Saurs published a second and a third edition of their Bible in 1763 and in 1776 respectively.

vians and the Sectarians had published hymn books. The Lutherans and the Reformed had also published catechisms. As early as 1746 Saur desired[363] to buy a copy of König's German and English Grammar in order to reprint it. In 1761 he published a biography of Frederick the Great.[364] In the same year Henrich Miller printed "Des Landmanns Advocat," a collection of useful extracts from various Pennsylvania and English laws.[365] He also published a "Wohl-eingerichtetes Vieh-Arzney-Buch" in 1771.[366] Aesop's fables were translated into German by G. F. Goetz, a German American, and published by Steiner and Kämmerer in 1794. This book was adorned with more than fifty copper engravings.[367] Probably the best seller of all non-religious German American books of the eighteenth century was a translation of William Cobbett's "The Bloody Buoy thrown out as a warning to the political pilots of America," published by Jungmann and Co., Reading, in 1797.[368] It was in reality a campaign document of the Federalist party and described the excesses committed in the French Revolution as a terrible warning to the American people. Jungmann boasted that he had sold between two and three thousand copies of it in less than three months.[369] Among the hundreds of other German books published in America, mention should be made of Teerstegen's "Geistiges Blumengärtlein inniger Seelen," which passed through seven editions between 1747[370] and

[363] S 76.
[364] S 4-24-61.
[365] S 1-29-62.
[366] M 472.
[367] PC₂ 313 ff.
[368] NUR 437.
[369] NUR 448.
[370] S 90.

1791,[371] of the Sectarian hymnal, "Das Kleine Davidische Psalterspiel," and of the journals of the Pennsylvania Assembly after 1786.[372]

The book importing business assumed large proportions at an early date. In 1772 seven hundred German books were offered for sale by one firm.[373] In the same year G. C. Reinholdt inserted in Miller's paper a full-page advertisement of imported books.[374] After the war almost every paper contained one or more book advertisements. In 1784 Robert Bell, of Philadelphia, announced that he had just received two hundred books from Germany.[375] Jacob Lahn, of Lancaster, published a two-page book advertisement in the *Lancäster Zeitung* of July 11, 1792.

Since it is impossible to name all the titles of the importations, I shall mention only some of those which are of interest to the literary historian. In 1754 "Flavius Josephus, jüdischer Geschichtschreiber" and Hubner's "Staats und Zeitungs Lexicon" were advertised.[376] In 1763 Peter Miller, of Philadelphia, offered[377] the following rather unusual books, "Begebenheiten dreyer Coquetten oder die Spaziergänge in dem Thuileries," "Wunderbare Avanturen zweyer lustigen Weltkinder," "Die vertauschten Kinder" and "Avanturen zweyer Frauenzimmer." The old German "Volksbücher" were apparently very popular throughout the entire century. For instance,

---

[371] NUL 190.
[372] GZ 27 et al.
[373] M 542.
[374] M 575.
[375] PC 165.
[376] S 164.
[377] M 66.

Anthon Armbrüster, of Philadelphia, sold[373] in 1764 "Die Historie vom Ewigen Juden." In 1767 Andreas Geyer, of the same city, advertised[379] "Kaiser Octavianus," "Die vier Haymonds Kinder," "Der listige Reineke Fuchs," "Das lustige und lächerliche Lalenbuch," "Eulenspiegel" and "Die schöne Melusina." That these books retained their popularity to the end of the century can be seen from two references to them: "Stoffel Ehrlich," of Conastoga township,[380] asserted in 1789 his belief in the truth of the "Faust" and "Der Ewige Jude" stories;[381] in 1797 the publisher of the *Readinger Zeitung* deprecated the popularity of such books as "Eulenspiegel," "Der gehirnte Siegfried," "Schöne Magelone" and "Genofefa."[382]

In the last two decades of the century many books written by contemporary German authors were imported, Goethe's "Werther" being apparently a particular favorite.[383] So great was the demand for German literature in 1783 that the Hamburg (Germany) firm of Thuun and Boden sent to Philadelphia a large assortment of books, among which were Goethe's,[384] Gellert's, Rabener's, Hagedorn's and Geszner's complete works, Klopstock's Messias, Hermannschlacht, odes and hymns, Ewald von Kleist's works, many of Wieland's works, Lessing's comedies and tragedies.[385] In the next year an English firm in Philadelphia, Robert Bell, imported, among others, Shake-

[378] M 144. There is some doubt whether this book was imported or published by Armbrüster.
[379] M 304.
[380] See above, p. 112.
[381] NUL 106.
[382] NUR 459.
[383] PC 129; NUL 4; DP 16 et al.
[384] In four volumes.
[385] PC 132.

speare's "Geist" and Klopstock's "Messias."[386] Beginning with 1790, Lancaster firms began to receive large shipments of books. Jacob Lahn offered for sale Gellert's, Rabener's and Klopstock's works,[387] Weisz's tragedies[388] (3 volumes), a German translation of Moliere's comedies,[388] the works[389] of Kleist, Geszner, Lessing, Goethe, Haller, Ramler, Meiszner, Michaelis, Hölty and Wieland. In 1799 Jacob Hütter, of Lancaster, received a large consignment of books from Germany, among which were Meusel's "Neues Museum für Künstler und Kunstliebhaber," Plank's "Romantische Erzählungen und Gedichte" and Goethe's "Wilhelm Meister's Lehrjahre" (4 volumes).[390] These advertisements, selected almost at random, may give some idea about the culture of the Pennsylvania Germans between 1780 and 1800. That the demand for books was widespread can not be doubted when we remember that there were German book stores in Easton, Reading, Lebanon, Harrisburg, York, Lancaster, Germantown, Chestnut Hill, Philadelphia and Baltimore. In Philadelphia alone there were at least eleven and probably many more at one time or another in the last eighteen years of the century.

The publications most widely read among the Pennsylvania Germans were undoubtedly the German almanacs. They contained, in addition to a calendar, many articles for instruction and entertainment. The contents of Miller's almanac for 1763 may be taken as a fair illustration of the contents of all of them. It contained, according to

[386] PC 151.
[387] NUL 169.
[388] NUL 202.
[389] NUL 227.
[390] DP 64.

the advertisement,[391] (1) Die Fluth oder das Hohe Wasser zu Philadelphia; (2) Die Reise des Lebens, Eine Sittenlehre; (3) Der Ungeratene Sohn. Ein schön Poetisch Stück; (4) Der Informator. Eine Poetische Erzählung; (5) Der tapfere Offizier. Ein Gedicht; (6) Merkwürdige Thaten, sinnreiche Urtheile und artige Einfälle des weltberühmten Herzogs von Ossuna, ehemaligen Vice-Königs in Sicilien und Neapolis; (7) Die Naturalisirungs Form derjenigen, welche Gewissens halben keinen Eid schweren können; (8) Eine zuverlässige Beschreibung der Insel Cuba, etc. The schedules of post riders, post wagons and ships were also printed in this almanac. More than twenty publishers issued almanacs at various times between 1750 and 1800. It is well known that Saur's "Der Hoch-Deutsch Americanische Calender" was exceedingly popular before the Revolution, but it is not so generally known that the rival Henrich Miller's "Der Neueste, Verbessert- und Zuverlässige Americanische Calender" was also sold by the thousands. In 1772 the supply did not equal the demand despite the fact that more than fifteen hundred copies had been printed.[392] In 1778, after the Saurs had left the city with the British, the demand for Miller's almanac was so great that he was required to print three editions. (John Dunlap's continuation[393] of the Saur almanac was apparently not very popular.) By 1800 almost every German newspaper publisher issued an almanac.

Although the Pennsylvania Germans of the eighteenth century did not possess many circulating libraries, some of them were quite famous. As early as 1766 the German town of Lancaster had a library company,[394] known as the

[391] M 38.
[392] M 469.
[393] M 897.
[394] S 371.

"Juliana Bibliothek Gesellschaft," which was still in existence twenty-one years later.[395] In 1785 Jacob Lahn started a "circulating library" in Philadelphia,[396] which in 1786 contained more than one thousand volumes of the best German authors.[397] Presumably this library was closed in the autumn of 1786 or early in 1787, for Lahn became a member of the firm which began the publication of the *Neue Unpartheyische Lancäster Zeitung* in August, 1787. In the spring of 1792 the "Mosheimische Gesellschaft"[398] of Philadelphia opened a German library.[399] It probably passed out of existence within a short time. In 1800 Christian Jacob Hütter, the publisher of the *Lancaster Correspondent*, established a circulating library in Lancaster. His terms were five dollars per year or one dollar and a half per quarter. He expected to be able to supply magazines and books three months after their publication in Germany.[400] In the issue of his paper of July 12, 1800, he announced the arrival in Philadelphia of four thousand books for his library. Hütter explained his reasons for starting the library in these words:

Ich suche nicht Eigennutz dabey, sondern wünsche Verbreitung nützlicher Kenntnisse, Aufrechthaltung der deutschen Sprache, Geschmack an Literatur dadurch zu bewirken, kurz ich wünsche meinen deutschen Freunden zu dienen, und zugleich müszige Stunden auf die angenehmste Art auszufüllen.[401]

In my attempt to describe the education and the educational facilities of the eighteenth century Pennsylvania

[395] NUL 7.
[396] PC 217, 224.
[397] PC 259.
[398] See Chapter on Language.
[399] PC₂ 157.
[400] H 36.
[401] H 40.

Germans, I am sure that the facts warrant the statement that these people were not without ideals in educational lines, that they were not as ignorant as has sometimes been stated, and that there was a continuous development in literary taste and in educational ideals. Granting that the aims of many of them, especially in the rural districts, were very narrow, nevertheless I believe that they compared very favorably with those of the descendants of other nationalities who were similarly located. If the leaders of a class of people saw so clearly the advantages of libraries and of schools, and made such earnest attempts to establish them, there was reason for optimism about their future development.

CHAPTER V.

LANGUAGE.

WHEN people leave their native country in order to settle in a land where the popular and official language is different from their own, the question always arises, whether they should attempt to preserve their native tongue, or whether it would be better for the general welfare to allow their posterity to be ignorant of the language in which their mothers sang lullabies to them. This question is bound to create dissensions not only among the immigrants themselves, but often also between them and their neighbors of other nationalities. Some of the immigrants will be convinced that it will be of advantage to their descendants and to the country to which they now owe allegiance, if all differences of language be erased as soon as possible. Others, however, viewing the extinction of their mother tongue with much the same emotion as one experiences on seeing the passing away of a dear lifelong friend, will insist that the only rational solution of the problem lies in learning the new language and at the same time preserving the old. Thus divisions arise among the settlers. The divisions between the immigrants and their neighbors are usually caused by the lack of a mutual sympathetic understanding. The neighbors are often suspicious of them, because different languages and customs, like an almost impassable gorge, separate them from one another. It is the purpose of this chapter to give an account of these dissensions.

Before I do this, however, I shall digress in order to consider the language which the immigrants spoke. Most of them were natives of South Germany, especially of the Palatinate, Württemberg and Switzerland.[402] Since almost all of them were peasants, it is logical to suppose that they used the dialect of their native locality and that the majority of them could speak the standard High German only with difficulty, if at all. I have been able to find only one specimen of a dialect in the papers.[403] A boy saw a dance for the first time and, rushing home to his father, described the fiddler and the dancers in the following words. "Dadi, was hun ich gseha!" "Was host du dan gseha?" "Ey ich hun a Ding gseha do isch a Kop druf und das bleckt die Zähn und der Man der zobelt dran, do knorrt's dan streicht er, do springa d'Leut in dem Haus rum und kaner kan die Thür finna." The dialect or dialects[404] had no written literature in the eighteenth century, so far as we know. They were not used by the press and the clergy and probably not by some of the others who had a good education.

[402] See Kuhns p. 115 ff. The newspapers mention the arrival of many shiploads of South German immigrants. Two references will have to suffice. In September 1749, Sauer reported that eight ships had just arrived with Swiss Württembergers, Palatines and Alsatians. In 1763 Miller announced the arrival of a ship at New York, containing two hundred and sixty Germans most of whom were from the Palatinate and Württemberg. (M 91.)

[403] NUR 272.

[404] The dialectical differences were gradually leveled, so that a new dialect, almost uniform throughout the entire Pennsylvania German district, appeared. This new dialect, the well known Pennsylvania German or "Dutch," has of course many English words. (See below.) At what period the new dialect appeared has not been definitely determined.

A dialect is prone to borrow words. This is probably due to various causes. In the first place, it has ordinarily a limited vocabulary, so that it is obliged to hunt for words to express new ideas. Again, since it has ordinarily no written literature, the dialect must be transmitted from individual to individual by word of mouth. Consequently, it does not possess a definite standard which might serve to prevent the intrusion of foreign words. After they have once been taken into the vocabulary of the dialect, it is only a question of time before they will begin to appear in the written language. Presumably the Germans in America soon began to use a considerable number of English words. Although the newspaper publishers attempted to use standard High German in their publications, we nevertheless find some English words in them. The English terms for objects which the Germans seldom or never saw in their native land or about which they were compelled to talk with their English neighbors appear often in the German newspapers. For instance, the following expressions are found in Saur's paper, Fens, Stoor, Zapling (sapling), Packet-Buch, Bille-Säl, Butscher, Schapkiper, Främ Haus, Seyder Press. In other (later) papers, such words are employed as Dieds, Livery Stall, Martgätsches, Lieses, Relieses, Klappbordfense, Pärtnerschip-Aufhebung, Cauärt, Summons, Trauar (drawer) and Hackbort.

This infusion of English words into the dialect became so pronounced that the newspapers after the Revolutionary War ridiculed the speech of the common people.[405] In 1784 the *Philadelphische Correspondenz* published[406] a

---

[405] It must be borne in mind that the following specimens are satires and, as such, probably exaggerate the use of English words. I believe that the proportion of English words found in the language of the common people was much less than in these articles.

[406] PC 183.

dialogue delivered before the "Deutsche Gesellschaft" on September 20, 1784, by three German students of Helmuth's Institute. In this dialogue one of them imitated the language of the uneducated. The following sentences have been taken almost at random from the satire. "Mit ihrer Deutschen Newspaper, warum lesen sie uns denn nicht rather diesen Artikel aus dem Englischen." "Einen Gentleman einen Thoren zu nennen, das ist meaner als mean; aber es nicht worth while, viel Notice davon zu nehmen, was sie sagen, because ich werde doch bleiben wer ich bin." "Dasz sie mich einen Fool schelten, denn das ist insufferable." "Wissen sie nicht dasz wir in ganz gepolischten Zeiten leben, in welchen sich unsere Attention mit wichtigen Objecten beschäftigen solten." "Es ist pitty, etc." Finally the speaker declared that he had spoken in this manner simply to make the others talk. One of them answered, "Ich dachte halb, dasz unser lustiger Freund nur spashaft seyn wolte, da er anfing den Pennsylvanischen Deutschen Dialect zu reden."[407]

About sixteen years later,[408] the same paper published a communication ridiculing the medley of languages which the Pennsylvania-Germans employed even in writing letters. It begins with the following introductory note to the publishers.

Herren Drucker,

Folgender in 1782 geschriebener Brief ist, wie ich höre, in Deutschland nach verschiedenen Universitäten geschickt worden,

---

[407] It is to be noted that the language of this satire and the following one is really a mixture of English and standard German, not of English and dialect German. There is, however, no reason to draw the conclusion from this that the language of ordinary conversation among the German Americans was standard German.

[408] PC. 29 (May 7, 1800).

ohne, dasz er, so hoch gelehrt die Herren auch sind, gehörig hätte erklärt werden können. Sie sehen, welchen Vorzug wir Americaner haben!

Then follows a letter ostensibly written by a lawyer to his client and friend. Of course, the legal terminology is entirely English, but in addition to this there are many other English words and idioms. The following are some of the most striking sentences. "Ihr müszt aber euren ganzen Cahs das nächste Mal in Reiting vorlegen." "Ich mankire nur noch eins zu wissen, ob eure hiesige Tenants gut nätjerd sind." "Ich glaube, ich will vor euch alles recoveren, und sonst euch einige Dienste erzeigen, dazu ich äbel bin." "Er hat grosze Lust zu travelen." "Ich weisz, ihr setzt viel Stohr auf ihn. Er hat einen grausamen Kopf für die Lerning. Es kommt keiner mit ihm auf." "Er war schon zweymal privatieren und hat zwey grosze Preisen nehmen helfen."

In 1792 the "Neue Unpartheyische Lancäster Zeitung" quoted from[409] Schöpf's "Reise," that the language of the Germans in Pennsylvania was a fearful mixture of German and English.

The first dissension on account of the language of the German immigrants arose, as may be expected, between the English and the Germans. The charity school movement has already been discussed[410] so that it is necessary here to emphasize only the reason why opposition developed. Many English feared that the Germans would hold themselves aloof from the other colonists, thus almost forming a commonwealth within a commonwealth, if they would not learn the English language;[411] the Germans, on

[409] NUL 261.
[410] See Chapter IV.
[411] S 9-1-54.

the other hand, resented this fear because they thought they could be just as loyal as the other nationalities who were permitted to retain their language without molestation. They also resented what they believed was an attempt to make their children forget their native tongue. They were probably almost unanimous in the desire to retain the language of their forefathers. Although Mühlenberg and Schlatter, the Lutheran and Reformed leaders, supported the charity school movement, they did so because they were convinced that the schools would help their countrymen to learn English and at the same time to preserve a knowledge of German.

The pamphlet mentioned above,[412] which was intended to describe conditions in Pennsylvania in 1754, indicates clearly how the Germans were misunderstood by their English neighbors. The author declared[413] that the Germans were so stupid that they could easily be misled by the French Catholics. He recommended that schools should be established for Germans, that English alone should be taught in them and that Germans should be disfranchised for twenty or thirty years until they could speak English. Although the author was apparently an extreme radical, his article clearly shows the great danger of dissension which may arise between neighbors speaking different languages.

From 1755 to 1781 the German papers are, with one exception, silent on the subject of language. We can, however, easily guess what was happening during this period,—undoubtedly the spirit of suspicion was gradually being replaced by one of mutual respect and goodwill. In the first place, the younger generation of both nationalities,

[412] See beginning of Chapter IV.
[413] S 184.

growing up side by side, appreciated one another better than their ancestors had done. This caused many prejudices to vanish. In the second place, this intimacy between the people presumably led to intermarriages, and such marriages were bound to be of great assistance in breaking down the barriers between the two nationalities. In the third place, an increasing number of Germans engaged in vocations[414] which compelled them to enter into business relations with the English element.[415] Business relations often create the most liberal tendencies. Each of the two parties began to perceive that the other party was composed of human beings having hopes and aims similar to their own. Moreover, the Germans noticed that a knowledge of English was absolutely necessary if they were to attain the business success which they desired. In the fourth place, the English and the Germans became a united people by the struggles and hardships which they had to endure in common. Beginning in 1765, when they stood shoulder to shoulder in fighting against the Stamp Act, which they considered a serious infringement upon their liberties, the two nationalities presented a united front during all the struggles culminating in the War for

[414] See Chapter VII.

[415] That the Germans began to feel the need of a knowledge of English can be seen from the English lessons printed by Henrich Miller in his newspaper in 1762. In announcing his intention of publishing a series of English lessons (M 25), he declared that the English language was as necessary in this country as commercial activity itself and as the association of one man with another. I may add that the phonetic values which Miller gives to some of the English letters are not above criticism; for instance, the sound of English "j" is made to correspond to German "dsch" (John-Dschon). He also declares that "th" is the veritable English shibboleth. He advises those Germans who cannot pronounce the sound correctly to pronounce it like "d," the symbol which he regularly uses for "th" in his lessons.

Independence. In this war the people of both parties shed their blood freely in a common cause, with the result that they became fused into a new nationality having common aims and ideals.[416]

When the Germans began to feel that they and their neighbors were so closely united by family, economic and national ties, they inevitably became more favorably disposed toward the English language. The prejudices against those who spoke English having largely disappeared, the process whereby the Germans would forget their own language and speak English only went on apace. This process of assimilation was accelerated by the fact that the official language of the State was English and by the corruption of the dialect or dialects discussed above. This corruption was increased by three factors. First, comparatively few Germans arrived in America between 1755 and 1781,—probably not more than twelve thousand.[417] Thus there were relatively few Germans in Pennsylvania who loved the German language on account of youthful associations connected with it, and whose speech had not been corrupted to a certain extent by the infusion of English words. Second, not only did this country receive very few immigrants but all intercourse with the old country was suspended for more than half a decade. Third, since English newspapers ordinarily printed the news sooner than the German, many Germans read the former only and almost forgot how standard High German looked. These three factors caused the dialect to become distinctly "Pennsylvania" German. Many of the common people, ridiculed by their English

---

[416] For a more detailed account of this struggle with the mother country, see Chapter VIII.

[417] See Kuhns, op. cit., p. 57.

friends and conscious that their language was far from being the German which their ministers were preaching in the pulpits, became ashamed of their dialect and attempted to speak the language which their English neighbors used.

These were the various influences which by 1781 had begun to threaten the extinction of the German language wherever the English population was mixed to any considerable extent with the German. Now the leaders of the religious denominations, the members of the "Deutsche Gessellschaft" and the German publishers attempted to check the tendency. This time the struggle was confined almost entirely to the Germans.

On August 29, 1781, the *Philadelphische Correspondenz"* published an article, signed "Ein Mitglied der deutschen Gesellschaft," in which the author lamented the fact that most of the young people of German extraction in Philadelphia read the English newspapers instead of the German. About one year later[418] another communication reported that many Germans were beginning to feel the need of the German language and to despise those Germans who showed no appreciation for it. In the dialogue mentioned above, which was given before the "Deutsche Gesellschaft" on September 20, 1784,[419] one of the speakers expressed his sorrow over the desire, evinced by many Germans of the rising generation, to become English. In 1787, we read a complaint that the city people consider the German language too coarse and consequently prefer a hundred times to talk poor English rather than good German and that they refuse to read German newspapers.[420] All these communications and complaints shed

[418] PC 83.
[419] PC 183.
[420] PC 304.

light upon the silent, gradual but apparently irresistible process which made the Germans English in speech.

Just as the Germans had united in the colonial days to effect an improvement in the condition of the immigrants, so they now began to make more systematic efforts for the preservation of their language. In 1788 the "Deutsche Gesellschaft" of Philadelphia, of which Melchior Steiner, the publisher of the *Philadelphische Correspondenz*, was secretary, offered a prize[421] for the best essay on the subject, "Wie kan die Aufrechthaltung und mehrere Ausbreitung der deutschen Sprache in Pennsylvanien am besten bewirket werden?" In the summer of 1789 the "Mosheimische Gesellschaft" was organized[422] by young men of German extraction for the purpose of learning the German language and of encouraging the people to use it in conversation.[423] The address delivered at the second anniversary of its founding is interesting because it indicates very plainly the aims of the society. The speaker bewailed the fact that so many of the descendants of German immigrants could not converse in German and were ashamed of their German-speaking brethren. The object of the society was to make people acquainted with the German language by urging the Germans to read it, to speak it, to think in it, to encourage others to speak it and to ridicule the German fool who was ashamed of his own language. Thus, the speaker declared, could German customs (Sitten) be preserved. The advantages of German customs were at least four in number: first, they made one popular; second, they assured peaceful days; third, they

---

[421] NUL 69.

[422] PC₂ 89; GZ₂ 61.

[423] I do not know whether this society was created at the instance of the "Deutsche Gesellschaft," but it seems very probable.

created wealth; fourth, they taught people to retain the wealth they had acquired.

In the spring of 1792 the society started a German library. When this was announced[424] in the *Philadelphische Correspondenz*, it created considerable discussion as to the advisability of attempting to preserve the German language in America. The argument was precipitated when a writer signing himself "Senex," who claimed to be a native of Germany, attacked[425] the library project and declared that the society would better sell its German books and buy English ones instead. He also said it would be better for the Germans if they would forget their own tongue and make English their only language. As conditions were, they could not talk English well and were consequently considered "Dummköpfe." Immediately a perfect avalanche of communications appeared, attempting to refute "Senex." In the issue of the following week[426] the paper published two of them. One of them claimed that the Germans could learn English so much the more readily if they knew German well. He cited examples to prove this. The other one simply ridiculed "Senex" without advancing any arguments. The next week[427] three more articles appeared. The first maintained that the Germans could be proud of their origin because that race had made itself the world's benefactor. The second called attention to the fact that the German Americans occupied prominent positions in our legislative bodies and that consequently not all of them were considered "Dummköpfe." The third advanced the argument that the Germans could easily

[424] PC_2 157.
[425] PC_2 164.
[426] PC_2 165.
[427] PC_2 166.

Language. 115

acquire both English and German, for many of them had learned not only these two but also French, Latin and Greek. The following week[428] the last two answers to "Senex" were published. The writer of one of them had apparently been very much hurt by the expression, "Dummköpfe." He hoped that the Germans would learn enough of both languages so that nobody would have any cause to speak of them in such derogatory terms. In the issue of July 31, 1792, "Senex" answered his opponents. He apparently considered only two arguments as meriting replies. He granted the truth of the statement that Germans could well be proud of what their nationality had done for the world, but asked of what practical value it was to American Germans even if Herschel, Händel and others were Germans. Such facts would not help them in their relations with their neighbors. He answered one of his opponents who claimed that a German could learn both languages by ridiculing the poor German which he had employed in his communication to the *Philadelphische Correspondenz*.[429]

Despite all attempts made by the Germans to preserve their language, their fight was a futile one. No human efforts could successfully counteract the aforementioned powerful influences. The Germans who desired the retention of the speech of their forefathers, often by being too conservative involuntarily assisted the tendency against

---
[428] PC$_2$ 167.
[429] This point probably forms the crux of the whole question of language. Those who advance the argument that it will do no harm for a group of people to learn two languages usually forget that the vast majority of people cannot, or at least do not, learn to speak two languages fluently and accurately. Thus one language will always remain foreign to them. I do not know how long the "Mosheimische Gesellshaft" remained in existence. I have found no mention of it after 1794. See PC$_2$ 328.

which they were fighting. The Lutheran leaders of Philadelphia did not include any English in the curriculum of their denominational schools, with the result that many German parents sent their children to English schools in order that they might learn English writing and counting.[430] Some of the most prominent German Americans did not encourage the newspapers published in the German language. For instance, F. A. Mühlenberg, son of the Reverend Heinrich Melchior Mühlenberg, and speaker of the first National House of Representatives, said in 1799 that he had only seldom seen German American newspapers during the past few years.[431] The German language had lost so much ground by 1800 that it seemed to some influential German Americans like a foreign language. A good example of this was Helmboldt, the publisher of the *Philadelphische Correspondenz*, who admitted that he was unable to write his articles in German but wrote them in English and had them translated.[432]

The process of anglicizing the speech of the Germans was naturally most active wherever they were continually meeting the English-speaking people, as for example in Philadelphia. However, in that large expanse of territory almost surrounding Philadelphia on the north, northwest, and west, that is in the counties of Northampton, Berks, Lancaster and York and parts of adjacent counties, where a traveler could probably journey for scores of miles without hearing anything but the dialect,[433] in this district the English language had made hardly any perceptible inroads upon the German. The dialect, even if

---

[430] See the articles by "Philoteutologos" discussed in Chapter IV.
[431] PC₃ 67.
[432] PC₃ 69.
[433] See PC 18.

not free from foreign words, was presumably much more nearly pure than in the territory contiguous to English settlements.

We can obtain various proofs that the German language was almost exclusively used in this territory occupied by the descendants of German immigrants. In 1787 the *Neue Unpartheyische Lancäster Zeitung* made the statement that almost everybody in Lancaster talked German.[434] The comparatively large circulation of German papers in the interior of Pennsylvania is another indubitable proof that a large proportion of the population spoke German. In 1781 the majority of the subscribers of the *Philadelphische Correspondenz* lived in the country districts.[435] In 1786 the *Germantauner Zeitung* had only one hundred and sixty subscribers in Philadelphia, while it had apparently many times that number in the rural districts.[436] The first German newspapers in Berks and Northampton antedated the first English newspapers of those counties by half a decade. The fact that small inland towns like Reading and Lancaster could support two German papers in 1800, poor though they were, while Philadelphia and vicinity with at least as large a German population and with its much higher culture could barely support two wretched sheets, permits us to draw a fairly accurate conclusion as to the relative use of the language in the interior as compared with Philadelphia. The large German book stores which were established in Lancaster between 1790 and 1800[437] also indicate that the German language was flourishing more there than in Philadelphia, where the German book trade was experiencing a noticeable decline.

[434] NUL 1.
[435] PC 18.
[436] GZ 27.
[437] See Chapter IV.

Thus the influences which were rapidly causing the German language to disappear in Philadelphia[438] had not yet seriously affected its vitality in German inland counties. Here the struggles for the preservation of the language were destined to be repeated during the entire nineteenth century, always with the same ultimate outcome,[439] so that now in the second decade of the twentieth century, the time seems not far distant when the last vestige of the remarkable Pennsylvania-German dialect will have vanished.

[438] The decline and virtual extinction of the German language in Philadelphia before 1820 is strikingly proved by a glance at the minutes of the "Deutsche Gesellschaft." This sturdy champion of German language and customs was compelled to bow to the inevitable in 1818, when it passed the following resolution. "Whereas inconveniences have been felt in keeping the records of this Society in the German language, therefore, resolved that all the proceedings of this Society be conducted in the English language." This resolution remained in effect up to 1859, with the exception that the two languages were on an equal footing between 1842 and 1849. In 1859 the German language was again restored to its former exclusive position. (See Seidensticker and Heinrici's *Geschichte der deutschen Gesellschaft von Pennsylvanien*, p. 65.) The reason for this recrudescence of German was probably the new tide of immigration to America in the thirties, late forties and early fifties. I may also add that there was no paper published in the German language in Philadelphia in 1820, so far as can be ascertained.

[439] An interesting sidelight on the gradual intrusion of English into the speech of the rural Pennsylvania Germans may be noted in the adoption of English or anglicized Christian names. At present, it is certain that more than ninety-nine per cent of the Christian names among the Pennsylvania Germans are English. When did the change commence? Among my own ancestors, my great-grandfather (born 1775) was called Johannes, but one of his younger brothers (born 1786) was named John Philip. All of my great-grandfather's children (born between 1805 and 1821) had English or anglicized names. Is not this change from German to English names highly suggestive of other great changes?

CHAPTER VI.

PENNSYLVANIA-GERMAN TRAITS.

ALMOST all of the characteristics of the Pennsylvania Germans may be explained as directly influenced by the deep piety of their forefathers and by certain qualities originating in the stern struggle for existence which they had experienced for centuries in Germany. To the former they chiefly owed their sterling moral qualities, their honesty and their obedience to the laws of the province, while their habits of industry, frugality and sobriety had undoubtedly been developed by the continual fight for existence under unfavorable circumstances.

Frugality is even at the present time a striking trait of the Pennsylvania Germans. It was very apparent in the eighteenth century, as may be seen from the references in the German newspapers. As we noted in another chapter,[440] the *Neue Unpartheyische Lancäster Zeitung* complained that the Germans refused to pay more than nine pence or one shilling for a book and that three or four German families clubbed together to buy a weekly newspaper at a dollar a year, while an English family was willing to pay twice as much for one. This paper also showed the frugality of its publishers when they attacked the use of snuff because it resulted in a waste of time and

[440] Chapter I.

money.[441] At another time this Lancaster publication without denying the truth of the allegation quoted Schöpf's "Reise durch America" to the effect that the German Americans hoarded their money and spent very little, even for the necessities of life.[442] When there was a general scarcity of currency in 1798, the *Deutsche Porcupein* blamed it partly upon the luxuriousness of the people who insisted on riding in public stage coaches when they could easily have saved the money by walking.[443] One of the favorite methods employed by politicians to arouse the Germans against the party in power was to raise the cry of extravagance. Thus, in 1793, an attack was made on a new law whereby the senators and assemblymen of Pennsylvania would receive three dollars a day instead of two as heretofore.[444]

This habit of economy was at least one of the reasons which caused the Germans to oppose the use of alcoholic drinks; of course, they also saw the danger of moral and physical deterioration from the excessive use of alcoholic stimulants. Feeling the need of temperance for such important reasons, the newspapers seized every opportunity to warn their readers against drunkenness, and gloried in the well-known sobriety of most of the Germans. In 1749 Saur urged the Germans not to spend so much money in hotels and public houses.[445] Eleven years later the second Saur expressed the wish that the importation of rum had been prohibited at the time of the founding of the colony.[446] After the war the papers published many articles against

[441] NUL 39.
[442] NUL 261.
[443] DP 2.
[444] NUR 227.
[445] S 3-1-49.
[446] S 3-28-60.

drunkenness.[447] In 1788[448] the Lancaster paper printed an interesting article describing a method which proved very successful in discouraging the use of whiskey. A farmer near Philadelphia, who offered to each harvester an additional sixpence a day instead of the customary whiskey, obtained so many helpers that his thirty-six acres of wheat were cut in one day. These numerous articles showing the folly and danger of over-indulgence do not prove that the Germans as a class had fallen into the habit. In fact there are definite and positive statements to the contrary in the newspapers. Two examples will suffice. In an article, signed "Philantropos," in the Lancaster paper, the author asserted that the Germans in America were less addicted to the use of strong drink than the people of any other nationality.[449] Some time later,[450] another communication was published in which the writer said that everybody around Pittsburg distilled and drank brandy and that now even some Germans of Lancaster had formed the habit. The writer regarded the danger as so serious that he demanded an impost of one dollar a gallon on rum, if it was impossible to stop the growth of the habit in any other way.[451]

Among the many newspaper articles,[452] praising the industry of the Germans, a good example is the one from Schöpf's "Reise," mentioned above, in which he says the Germans are noted for their industry.[453] Their frugality, as well as their industry in the colonial days is nowhere

[447] NUL 4, 54, 80; PC 89, 91, 381 et al.
[448] NUL 52.
[449] NUL 55.
[450] NUL 60.
[451] It is to be noted that the writers of these articles saw no harm in beer.
[452] NUL 55, 261; NUR 530; PC 20, 121 et al.
[453] NUL 261.

better illustrated than in an article published[454] in 1786 in which the economy of the Germans of forty years ago is contrasted with the contemporary desire for the luxuries of life. The correspondent says that, at the age of twelve, he was given by his parents to a farmer, with whom he lived up to the age of twenty-one. On attaining his majority the farmer gave him two suits of homespun clothes, four pairs of socks, four linen shirts and two pairs of shoes. This was all the capital which he possessed at the time. At twenty-two he married and rented a farm of forty acres. Ten years later he bought a farm of sixty acres. Now he began to make money and gradually acquired more land. When his oldest daughter married he gave her one hundred acres of land and some of his best flax, so that she could spin cloth for herself. At this time he was saving one hundred and fifty dollars a year because he spent no money unnecessarily. Deducting the taxes, he did not spend ten dollars yearly, and this he was compelled to spend in order to procure the necessities of life, such as salt, nails, etc. He bought cattle, fattened and sold them, and put his money out at interest. Then the change in the mode of living occurred. When his second daughter married, his wife *bought* kitchen utensils for her. His third daughter wore silk dresses. The spinning wheel was scarcely ever used, as the family bought the material for clothes. All these purchases made his expenses higher than his income.

This extreme thrift which begrudged the spending of a single cent for anything but the barest necessities did not extend to the erection of buildings or to food. The canny Germans probably knew that good and sufficient food and substantial buildings were absolutely necessary for their continued success. Hence Schöpf could say that no class

[454] PC 285.

of people in Pennsylvania had warmer houses or better fences than the Germans and that they also had fine barns.[455] As early as 1749, Saur declared that the Germans lived in good dwellings and even palaces.[456] In 1795 a farm in Strassburg, Lancaster County, was offered for sale, having the following improvements: a stone house two stories high, with four rooms on each floor, two cellars and a porch; a kitchen, attached to the house; a well and pump; a log house; a barn with stables.[457]

The newspapers were silent about the food of these thrifty peasants, although the press attacked the custom of having big feasts at funerals and baptisms. Saur was opposed[458] to the custom because many became drunk at the funeral feasts. He hoped that all would follow the example of some influential people who had abandoned the custom. More than forty years later, Gottlob Jungmann printed[459] an article in his paper denouncing the custom of eating at funerals and baptisms, because the expenses were too heavy and because it was not sanitary to eat on the former occasions.

The Germans in America were generally scrupulously honest. In addition to the remarkable conscientiousness of Saur, which I have already mentioned,[460] other examples of honesty are noted in the papers. In 1784 the *Philadelphische Correspondenz* said that the Germans in Pennsylvania had the reputation of paying their debts.[461] The people of Berks County were so honest and peaceable that

[455] NUL 261.
[456] S 3-1-49.
[457] NUR 311. This farm was probably quite typical of those at the close of the century.
[458] S 140.
[459] NUR 386.
[460] See Chapter I.
[461] PC 183.

the only inmates of the county jail in Reading for at least two months in 1789 were the jailor and his family.[462] Naturally there were also instances of dishonesty, and more of these are recorded in the papers than examples of honesty, simply because the former possessed more general interest as news items. In the middle of the century, when counterfeiting was very prevalent, we find at least two instances of the conviction of Germans for that crime.[463] Another case of dishonesty[464] is that of Heinrich Merckel, tax collector of Earl Township, Lancaster County, who absconded in 1789. While the cases of gross dishonesty were undoubtedly very rare, a much more sweeping charge was made in a letter, written in 1787, which complained of widespread dishonesty, especially among the farmers with regard to weights and measures.[465] The papers also contained numerous advertisements offering rewards for the apprehension of runaway German redemptioners. Although the indentured servants may at times have been justified in breaking their contracts, the frequency of these occurrences is almost conclusive proof that not all of the servants were honest.

On the subject of sexual immorality it is even more difficult to draw general conclusions from the newspapers. We have already seen[466] how Saur attacked some of the early Lutheran and Reformed ministers on the ground of immorality. Such immorality was, however, by no means restricted to the ministers, who as a class undoubtedly improved when better men could be imported. The inland German newspapers of the last ten years of the century

[462] NUR 23.
[463] S 99, 11-1-51.
[464] NUL 105.
[465] NUL 6.
[466] See Chapter II.

contained many advertisements which were inserted by young bridegrooms denying that they were the fathers of the children on whose account the law had compelled them to marry the mothers. Husbands often inserted advertisements notifying the merchants that they did not intend to pay any debts contracted by their runaway wives. Adultery was the usual cause assigned for these desertions. Although the condition of affairs depicted in the papers would seem serious, we must remember that we have no means of estimating how widespread fornication was, because the editors never thought of publishing any instances of virtuous husbands and wives. We may be confident that sexual vice was the exception rather than the rule.[467]

Since the Pennsylvania Germans were frugal and pious, we may be curious to know in what kinds of amusements, if any, they indulged. While we may assume that their recreation was of a simple kind, the newspapers do not enlighten us on this point. They do, however, attack various forms of amusement, such as dancing, theatrical performances and the celebration of New Year's Eve by the shooting of firearms. The last named practice was strongly condemned by the older Saur, who is the authority for the statement that "New Year's shooting" was very common among the Germans.[468] Saur's attacks on dancing were at times naïve. For instance, after the account of the reception given the Governor of Maryland at Baltimore, at which there was a dance, Saur added that he hoped that the Governor had not danced because it would have set a bad example.[469] The condemnation of theatrical per-

[467] For a particularly unfavorable and prejudiced account of the alleged immorality of the Germans, see Gottlieb Mittelberger's "Reise nach Pennsylvania im Jahr 1750."
[468] S 152.
[469] S 166.

formances was much more general than the attacks on dancing, the latter coming chiefly from the Dunker papers. When a playhouse was being built in Philadelphia in 1766, the *Staatsbote* joined the English papers in a determined opposition to the project. The announcement was made from the Lutheran and Reformed pulpits that the various religious denominations, both English and German, had united to send a protest against the playhouse to the provincial governor.[470] In 1789 the Lancaster paper also showed its disapprobation of plays when it reported that young boys in Germany were led to form a band of robbers by reading Schiller's "Räuber."[471] Samuel Saur asserted[472] that tragedies and comedies were written for the purpose of entertaining vain people.[473]

The attempt in this chapter to show some of the leading traits of the German immigrants and their descendants is at best unsatisfactory, because, for such a subject, newspapers are usually unreliable as sole sources of material. This is especially true concerning the discussion of the vices and the criminal tendencies of the people. To illustrate this, let the reader peruse a newspaper of the present day; he will discover that much of the news relating to the subject deals with extravagances, divorces, robberies and murders. What a dark picture could a person, reading these items two centuries hence, draw concerning our times!

[470] M 264.
[471] NUL 98.
[472] CW 104.
[473] Theatres are anathema to many of the rural Pennsylvania Germans even at the present day. For example, I have heard a dear old lady say that Abraham Lincoln was the most immoral president that we ever had. Her conviction was based on the fact that he was shot in that devil's resort, a theatre.

CHAPTER VII.

VOCATIONS OF THE EIGHTEENTH CENTURY PENNSYLVANIA GERMANS.

WHEN we turn to the subject of the vocations of the eighteenth century Germans, we discover that the latter were engaged in a great variety of occupations. Almost every conceivable trade is mentioned in the advertisements, while the news sections of the papers show us that the Germans also held responsible positions in the learned professions, two of which, teaching and preaching, have already been discussed.[474]

Since most of the Pennsylvania Germans had been tillers of the soil in the old country and since the greater number lived in the rural districts in America, agriculture was naturally the occupation in which most of them were engaged. They seem to have been particularly interested in fruit growing and dairying. Of the hundreds of advertisements offering farms for sale, there are very few which do not impart the information that the farm to be sold contains fine pasture land and possesses a flourishing orchard. As an instance of the former, a sentence from an advertisement in the *Neue Unpartheyische Lancäster Zeitung* furnishes a good example—"No piece of land can have a location more favorable for the raising of cattle."[475] The

[474] See Chapters II and IV.
[475] NUL 13.

German settlers unquestionably enjoyed an enviable reputation as successful dairymen. Sometimes the most liberal inducements were offered to them to take charge of a wealthy man's herd. Thus, in 1772, a dwelling house, firewood and three acres of land for a garden were promised to a satisfactory German couple who knew how to take care of six or seven cows and make butter.[476] The orchards generally contained apple, cherry and peach trees, and occasionally also pear trees and grape vines. For instance, one orchard with seventy young apple trees was advertised,[477] another one with early and late cherry and peach trees,[478] a third one with three hundred apple and five hundred peach trees,[479] a fourth one with one hundred apple trees,[480] a fifth one with cherry, peach, pear and apple trees, and ten grape vines.[481]

Of course, the farmers sowed wheat, barley and corn. The great importance of the wheat crop in the eyes of the German farmers is proved by the numerous newspaper articles[482] discussing ways and means of combating the depredations of the dangerous Hessian flies, with which the country was so grievously afflicted in the eighties and nineties. The newspapers do not make any estimates of the number of bushels of wheat raised yearly, but the exportation from Philadelphia in 1797 of one hundred and thirty-six thousand three hundred and thirty barrels of flour[483] enables us to form a good idea of the size of the

---

[476] M 545.
[477] S 38.
[478] S 81.
[479] S 87.
[480] NUL 89.
[481] PZ 63.
[482] NUL 53, DP 34, et al.
[483] DP 2.

wheat crop, since it is fairly certain that much of the wheat from which the flour was made came from the hinterland occupied by the Germans.[484]

Although the Germans were successful in raising crops, they were never satisfied and were continually attempting to improve their methods. It is very suggestive that two of the German newspapers most widely read between 1785 and 1790, the *Germantauner Zeitung* and the *Neue Unpartheyische Lancäster Zeitung*, contained so many articles on farming subjects that we may almost regard these papers as the forerunners of our present-day agricultural journals. The former paper published articles on the value of lime for the soil,[485] on the superiority of oxen over horses as draught animals,[486] on the value of manure,[487] concerning orchards[488] and potatoes[489] and a series of articles on methods of farming.[490] In the Lancaster paper the value of gypsum for increasing the fertility of the soil was discussed at length,[491] a communication about the grasses most suitable for fodder was published[492] and an article appeared,[493] showing the necessity of performing careful experiments in order to determine what agricultural methods would produce the best results and declaring that higher schools and societies would be a great help in conducting the tests. Later the paper published an article urging the

[484] The papers also mention the raising of pigs, horses, sheep and geese.
[485] GZ 61.
[486] GZ 62.
[487] GZ 65.
[488] GZ 67, 68.
[489] GZ_2 44.
[490] GZ_2 58 ff.
[491] NUL 4, 5, 15, 18, 38.
[492] NUL 6, 10.
[493] NUL 72.

people to raise sheep[494] and another one telling them how to make butter in winter.[495] In 1790 the *Neue Unpartheyische Readinger Zeitung* contained an article[496] describing a model barn and barn yard as set forth in a paper by George Morgan, of Princeton, New Jersey, which had won a prize offered by the Philadelphia Society for the Encouragement of Agriculture. It is of course a question how many farmers attempted to put into practice the improvements suggested in these articles, just as it is a question how many farmers of the present day really make use of the improvements discussed in the agricultural papers; but the very fact that so many articles were published leads us inevitably to believe that there was a demand for them and that the farming population was not satisfied with the old when the new gave promise of something better.

As good and bad was found in the consideration of the education, religion and characteristics of the eighteenth century Germans, so in their farming they showed faults mingled with their virtues. Many of them were firmly convinced that the moon and the stars had a decisive influence on the success or failure of crops. A very interesting communication, illustrating this belief, appeared in the *Germantauner Zeitung* of July 24, 1787. The writer advised the farmers to take the phases of the moon and the signs of the zodiac into consideration when planting, and suggested that, since the Germans had always done this and were generally acknowledged to be without superiors in gardening, it might be well to publish a treatise on the subject. He begged his readers not to ridicule the belief in the influence of heavenly bodies but to try the following

[494] NUL 96.
[495] NUL 241.
[496] NUR 54.

experiment with a mind as free as possible from prejudice: let some peas be planted in the waxing moon and others in the waning moon. The writer claimed that the plants from the former would bloom well and bear abundantly, while those from the latter would indeed bloom well but would not produce many peas.[497]

Interested as the Pennsylvania Germans were in agriculture, they naturally turned their attention to the manufacture of agricultural implements and other articles that the farmers needed. In 1770 Adam Eckhart, a maker of chaff separators, said in an advertisement in the *Staatsbote* that he had made more than sixteen hundred during his life.[498] Manufacturers of whetstones,[499] harvest cradles,[500] scythes[501] and sickles[502] are also mentioned. Many saw mills and grist mills were operated by the Germans all over the country. The former[503] were usually located on big farms, while the latter[504] were found in every vicinity, both in town and in country.

Of the company that established the first permanent German settlement in Germantown in 1683, the majority were weavers.[505] The raising of flax and the weaving of cloth continued to be an important industry among the

[497] This superstition, according to some writers, may not have been quite as useless as it seems at first sight, since it may have resulted in their giving close attention to the weather conditions of the country and therefore may have been an aid to their success. (See Faust's "German Element in the United States," Vol. I, p. 137, on Benjamin Rush's pamphlet on the Pennsylvania Germans.)

[498] M 447.
[499] *E.g.*, NUL 9.
[500] DP 20.
[501] DP 20.
[502] e.g., PC 213.
[503] NUL 38, 77; M 419 and many other places.
[504] S 43, 2-15-60, 9-25-61, M 217, 419, PC 124, 148, PC, 41 et al.
[505] See Faust's "German Element," Vol. I, p. 37.

Germans during the entire eighteenth century. Thus we find advertisements by a stocking-weaver[506] and a linen weaver[507] in Saur's paper, and occasionally looms were offered for sale.[508] An idea of the magnitude of the weaving business among the Germans in 1770 can be gained from a letter written to the American Philosophical Society and reprinted in the *Staatsbote*.[509] It gives an itemized account of the cloth woven in the city of Lancaster alone between May, 1769, and May, 1770, the total amounting to twenty-seven thousand seven hundred and ninety-three yards with an additional six or seven thousand yards still on the looms and sufficient yarn in the houses to weave one thousand yards more. In the colony of Georgia the German Salzburgers, who lived at Ebenezer, were also engaged in weaving, although they complained of a lack of weaving implements. They generally mixed flax with cotton yarn, thus making cloth that was very strong. The Salzburgers also raised silk. The hundred families in the settlement produced six thousand seven hundred and two pounds in 1762, six thousand three hundred and two pounds in 1763 and six thousand four hundred and ninety-one pounds in 1764.[510] The Revolutionary War apparently almost completely paralyzed the weaving industry of Pennsylvania. However, shortly after the close of the war, it again rose into importance. In 1788 and 1789 two Philadelphia firms sold five thousand six hundred and eighty spinning wheels.[511] The Lancaster paper urged the

[506] S 138.
[507] S 3-1-55.
[508] e.g., S 59, 94.
[509] M 439.
[510] M 163.
[511] NUL 98.

farmers to raise more flax in 1788.⁵¹² The Moravians at Lititz, Lancaster County, owned a weaving establishment in 1787.⁵¹³

As a necessary adjunct to weaving, fulling mills were erected wherever the industry flourished. In fact, I believe that the newspapers contained more advertisements of fulling mills than of anything else except merchant wares and real estate. These mills were scattered through the counties of Lancaster, Berks, Bucks and Northampton.⁵¹⁴

After the cloth was finished, it could be taken to people of German descent who made a regular business of dyeing. According to the advertisements,⁵¹⁵ dyers dwelled in all of the principal towns, such as Philadelphia, Germantown, Reading, Lancaster, Harrisburg and Bethlehem. In the last mentioned place Joseph Barth in 1774 printed calico and linen in colors which, he claimed, were as fast as any to be found in Europe.⁵¹⁶ In 1791 Pfaffhauser and Schwab conducted a calico printing and bleaching establishment in Philadelphia.⁵¹⁷

Workers in metals were by no means rare. Iron was manufactured from an early date.⁵¹⁸ Nail makers,⁵¹⁹ locksmiths,⁵²⁰ blacksmiths,⁵²¹ tinsmiths,⁵²² coppersmiths⁵²³ and brass founders⁵²⁴ were plentiful. The manufacture of

---

[512] NUL 35.
[513] NUL 14.
[514] *E.g.*, S. 42, 44, 2-15-60; M 93; NUL 6, 63, 225.
[515] *E.g.*, S 2-1-53, 3-1-55; M 260, 675; PC₂ 401; A 10, 11; UH 45.
[516] M 658.
[517] PC₂ 95.
[518] S 9-1-49.
[519] NUL 93; A 116 et al.
[520] DP 16; H 62 et al.
[521] S 6-1-51; NUR 111 et al.
[522] S 178; NUR 156 et al.
[523] S 8-1-54; NUR 559 et al.
[524] UH 4.

stoves, wire, needles and pins is recorded.⁵²⁵ Christoph Saur, the first, was interested in a new kind of stove of which he was probably the inventor. In his paper of September 1, 1749, he announced the manufacture at the Reading Furnace of a new stove, which could be examined at his printing establishment in Germantown. The advertisement claimed that such a stove would heat a large room and that cooking, frying and baking could be done on the stove without spreading an odor through the room. The famous iron foundry of Henrich Wilhelm Stiegel at Mannheim, Lancaster County, and its products were not specifically described in the papers, unless I have overlooked it; but his glassware was mentioned. In 1771 Stiegel showed to the American Philosophical Society specimens of glassware made at his factory, which was the equal of any foreign-made glass.⁵²⁶

The manufacture of hats, paper and gunpowder deserves special mention because the making of them was to a large extent in the hands of the Germans and was chiefly restricted to certain localities. In the last decade of the century Reading was the great centre of the hat industry.⁵²⁷ Most of the paper mills in Pennsylvania were located in the vicinity of Philadelphia, and many of them were owned and operated by Germans.⁵²⁸ The powder mills which were run by Germans were generally close to Philadelphia.⁵²⁹

[525] M 713; PC 127.
[526] M 493.
[527] PC 437; NUR 127, 299 et al.
[528] S 11-1-51; M 177, 680; PC 117; PC₂ 543; NUR 58 et al.
[529] S 235; M 767; PC 146; NUL 262, 279; PC₂ 152. Many of these references are not advertisements but accounts of accidents. Thus PC 146 announces the blowing up of a powder mill. Explosions with fatalities are reported in the mills of Keiser (NUL 262), Losch (NUL 279), Herzel (PC₂ 152).

I shall pass over most of the other industries with but slight mention, although some of them were undoubtedly important. The papers refer to sugar factories[530] in Philadelphia, to a chocolate factory[531] in Lancaster, to breweries,[532] to whiskey distilleries,[533] of which there were only a few, to tanneries,[534] to a turpentine distillery,[535] to the manufacturing of potash,[536] brooms and brushes,[537] ropes,[538] pumps[539] and pottery.[540] Many clock and watch makers were found throughout the entire German district.[541] For instance, Saur's paper had an advertisement by two of them, one of whom had learned the trade in Nuremberg and the other in Philadelphia.[542] Among the Pennsylvania Germans of the eighteenth century, there were also saddlers, shoemakers, tailors, wood carvers, butchers, carpenters, jewelers, masons, coopers, wheelwrights, wagon-makers, bakers, stone-cutters and charcoal burners. The advertisements of many printers and book binders are also found in the various newspapers.

One of the most noteworthy industries which made the Germans famous throughout the length and breadth of the land was the manufacture of musical instruments. Most of these skilled artisans lived in Lancaster County and in

[530] S 3–17–59, 256; PC 333, 369.
[531] DP 11.
[532] S 78; M 593; NUR 81; A 100 et al.
[533] M 62, 667, NUL 36; A 150.
[534] S 137; M 65, 177; PC 65; NUL 208.
[535] M 448.
[536] DP 50.
[537] NUL 16, 82; NUR 22.
[538] NUR 496.
[539] M 336.
[540] S 203.
[541] S 139; M 115, 338; NUL 208; DP 3; NUR 3, 127; A 26, 128; H 63; UH 32, etc.
[542] S 165.

Philadelphia. In 1762 Philip Fyring, a German by birth, who had come to this country several years before, built an organ for Saint Paul's church of Philadelphia.[543] Evidently Fyring (or Feyering) was widely famed for his skill, for he was later compared with the most famous organ builder of Pennsylvania, David Tanneberg(er) of Lititz, Lancaster County. This latter artist began to build organs in America without any previous apprenticeship, but by reading, meditation and unflagging zeal became such an expert that he was claimed in 1790 to be the equal of the most skilled organ builder of Europe.[544] The first mention of him which I have discovered in the newspapers was in 1771, when he built an organ for the Reformed church of Lancaster. The organ was highly praised for the quality of its tone and it was asserted to be superior to the organs made by the deceased Feyering.[545] In 1790 Tanneberg completed his famous organ for Zion's Lutheran Church of Philadelphia.[546] In the winter of 1798-99 he built one for the Moravian church in the city of Lancaster.[547] He died suddenly in 1804, as he was completing an organ in a York church.[548] Lancaster County was undoubtedly the great centre for the manufacture of musical instruments. As early as 1763, George Schlosser of Lancaster was offering pianos for sale.[549]

[543] M 50.
[544] NUL 168; PC₂ 4.
[545] M 482.
[546] See Chapter II.
[547] DP. 56.
[548] AS 336 (May 30, 1804.) According to an article in the *Pennsylvania German Magazine* (Vol. X, p. 339) by A. R. Beck, the archivist of the Moravian church at Lititz, Tanneberg was born in Upper Lusatia, Germany on March 21, 1728. The author mentions twenty seven organs built by Tanneberg for various churches.
[549] M 79.

After the war the town of New Holland became noted as the home of constructors of musical instruments. The manufacture of organs, pianofortes, spinets, pianos and hand organs in this town was advertised in 1788.[550] At the same time a certain Johann Scheible(y) of New Holland was advertising extensively as an organ builder.[551]

There are few instances on record in the papers that the Pennsylvania Germans manufactured scientific instruments. In the winter of 1790-1791 Jacob Welschantz, a celebrated gunsmith of York, made a very good air pump under the supervision of Mr. Heterich, who had formerly been an instructor in the York Academy.[552] In 1771 David Rittenhouse,[553] probably the most famous astronomer that has come from Pennsylvania German stock, made an orrery, which was taken to Princeton on April 9, 1771, where it was set up.[554]

For the distribution and exchange of the varied manufactures of the Germans, merchants were needed. In the early period there were many itinerant peddlers who carried their wares all over the country.[555] Their numbers probably decreased with the establishment of regular stores in the rural districts; at least, the number of merchants in-

[550] NUL 68.
[551] NUL 75; PC 206.
[552] NUR 122; PC$_2$ 71.
[553] This is the celebrated Rittenhouse who made important observations on the transit of Venus in 1769. He was also treasurer of the state of Pennsylvania for a number of years. At the time of his death in 1796, he was president of the American Philosophical Society, the organization made famous by Benjamin Franklin, who had been its founder and president. Dr. Benjamin Rush a distinguished Philadelphia physician, delivered the eulogy on Rittenhouse's death. See PC$_2$ 526. It should be noted that Rittenhouse was of German-Dutch extraction.
[554] M 482.
[555] S 33; LZ 12 et al.

creased more rapidly than the number of peddlers. Almost every issue of the German papers, published toward the close of the century, contained one or more advertisements by German merchants. Without making by any means an exhaustive study of the subject, I have counted thirty-five German merchants in Philadelphia between 1782 and 1801, and fifteen in Berks County between 1789 and the end of the century. Among these are included grocers, and dry goods and hardware merchants. Some of these merchants had a very high standing in the community; for instance, Heinrich Keppele, Sr., of Philadelphia became the first president of the "Deutsche Gesellschaft" of that place; Friederich Augustus Mühlenberg, who owned a store at Trappe in 1783,[556] later became the speaker of the first national House of Representatives; a Joseph Hiester, a merchant at Reading in 1789,[557] was probably the same man who afterwards became governor of Pennsylvania. There were also many German hotel proprietors[558] and some wholesale liquor dealers[559] and wine merchants.[560] In 1799 a seed house in Philadelphia was owned by Daniel Englemann.[561]

I have discussed in earlier chapters the Pennsylvania Germans as teachers and ministers. Very few of them studied law, probably being deterred by a number of reasons: the fact that so few had a good command of the English language was a serious drawback to their legal aspirations, if they had any; then again some of them may have also felt an aversion to law similar to that expressed

[556] PC 134.
[557] NUR 36.
[558] M 499, 580 etc.
[559] *E.g.*, M 71.
[560] M 898 et al.
[561] PC₂ 33.

by Saur. The Pennsylvania Germans could, however, boast of a considerable number of druggists and physicians.[562] We have seen[563] how one of the former, Johann Kühmle, remained in Philadelphia during the yellow fever epidemic of 1793. He was apparently a well-educated man with a scientifically trained mind, as we may conclude from two articles by him on the origin of the epidemic.[564] In these he disagreed with those medical men who claimed that the fever had been caused by the very dry hot weather and the filth of the city. He showed that the former had been prevalent over the whole country during the summer months and the latter was common in the city every summer. He expressed the belief that the fever was "imported wares." The German physicians had either studied in Europe[565] or had served a kind of apprenticeship in this country[566] with one of the practicing physicians. Although the qualifications were certainly not high, physicians remained so scarce that some communities were not supplied as late as 1773, in which year the town of Lebanon (which contained two hundred and fifty families at the time) advertised for a doctor. A knowledge of the German language was one of the first qualifications for this particular position because all of the inhabitants were Germans.[567]

The fact that stands out prominently in a study of the newspapers of the period is that the Germans entered almost all industries and professions with zest and success.

[562] S 165, 236; M 272, 580; PC 47, 67, 348; PC$_2$ 540; NUR 365; NUL 80 etc.
[563] See Chapter III.
[564] PC$_2$ 256.
[565] DP 85, M 135.
[566] DP 70.
[567] M 592.

They were most prominent as farmers, but by no means did they restrict their activities to this pursuit. They were millers, weavers, carpenters, wagon builders, merchants, tradesmen, manufacturers of musical instruments, of iron, glass and pottery.

CHAPTER VIII.

POLITICAL IDEALS.

SINCE the Pennsylvania Germans were thrifty and peace loving they necessarily must have been a class of people who would have added to the wealth and stability of any country. However, domestic virtues are not the only ones essential to a high class citizen, he must also possess an active and intelligent interest in public affairs. It is on account of their supposed indifference to, or ignorance of, the larger aspects of public welfare that the Pennsylvania Germans have been most severely criticized. I intend to show in this chapter what conception these eighteenth century German Americans had with regard to government and to national politics, and what their attitude was to provincial and national events from 1740 to 1801.

Their most striking characteristic as citizens was their intense love of liberty, the expression of which ran like a golden thread through almost all their newspapers. Thus in 1754 Saur reported[568] the following event: a native of Württemberg, on being asked why so many Germans had risked the long and dangerous voyage to this country, replied that they had come because they had scarcely been able to live in Germany, owing to governmental oppression; of course, he added, they could have gone to Prussia,

[568] S 12-1-54.

which had offered them inducements, but there they would have been slaves and vassals. This same love for liberty is shown in Henrich Miller's refusal[569] to stop printing communications which contained attacks on individuals; he declared that he did not want to deny the use of his paper to anyone who had something to say, because the freedom of the press was the bulwark of liberty.

After the war the newspapers seized upon many opportunities to proclaim the idea of liberty. For instance, on the statement that the Czarina, the Emperor and the Turks possessed many thousands of soldiers, one editor commented as follows: "Horrible thought! that the lives of so many men must be at the command of an arbitrary mortal, or that, at the present day, religion must serve as the cloak for such bloody scenes."[570] Again, another editor in 1791 bitterly attacked a part of the letter sent by the pope to his legate in Paris on July 30, 1790, in which the pope talked about "the principles of independence and liberty which the enemies of all religion, of all thrones and of all public order disseminate." The editor answered, "Not much is gained by lying and slandering, and the Holy Father should be ashamed to call those who spread the principles of independence and liberty, enemies of religion and good order."[571]

In 1794 the *Philadelphische Correspondenz* published[572] the following poem, "An die Americaner."

> 1. Wie schlägt mir mein Herz so hoch,
> Ich athme freye Luft,
> So schlägt es, wenn in schwüler Zeit
> Ein kühles Lüftgen mich erfreut,
> Gemischt mit Rosenduft!

[569] M 229.
[570] NUL 44.
[571] PC$_2$ 10.
[572] PC$_2$ 266.

2. Wie ruht sich doch so süsz, so süsz
   Der Freyheit in dem Schoos,
Mein Blut fliesztt leicht, und froh, und schnell,
Mein heiteres Auge blickt so hell,
   Mein Herz ist sorgenlos!

3. Hier wo die Freyheits Fahne weht,
   Wo die Vernunft gebeut,
Wo jeder, als ein freyer Mann,
Frey sprechen, glauben, würken kan:
   Hier ist die güldene Zeit!

4. Hier gilt kein Ordensstern, noch Band,
   Ja selbst kein schwarz Gewand,
Nur der ist grosz und hoch geehrt,
Der Redlichkeit im Busen nährt,
   Und liebt sein Vaterland!

5. Du zeigest, braves, freyes Volk,
   Was Menschenkraft vermag,
Was Wuth and Unvernunft zerbricht,
Und durch die Kraft der Wahrheit siegt,
   Und so sein Gück erzielt

6. Heil dir, du edles freyes Volk!
   Ich, Fremdling, neide dich,
In meinem Deutschen Vaterland
Bist du verschrien und verkannt,
   O kennt es dich, wie ich!

This poem expresses the passionate love of liberty that animated so many of the Germans who came to these shores in the eighteenth century.[573]

The conviction that they enjoyed more personal liberty in their new home than they had possessed in their old one, made the Germans devoted to the new country. For ex-

---

[573] This poem is presumably a genuine German American production, although many of the poems which appeared in the papers anonymously were copied from German sources. This one, however, is headed, "Für die Philadelphische Correspondenz." It is the best eighteenth century German American poem which I have seen.

ample, Saur said[574] that they should love America because they lived in much greater comfort here, having no more feudal services to render and enjoying freedom of religion and of conscience. In 1758 the second Saur declared that his father had always attempted to work for the best interest of his adopted home and that no partisan attacks had ever made him act contrary to this principle.[575] We have seen in another chapter[576] how Miller praised the country. Reiche in his *Postbothe* gave[577] very high praise to the land and its government, calling the former a paradise.

Knowing that a government which granted such personal liberties to its subjects could not exist unless the people showed an intelligent interest in the public welfare, the German leaders from the beginning attempted to arouse in their countrymen an intelligent appreciation of the laws and to induce them to participate actively in public affairs. Thus, the first issue of the first German paper published in America contained the promise of the editor to print the laws of the province.[578] In 1743 Saur published in his paper the charter of Pennsylvania in order that people might learn what liberty the King of England and Penn had bestowed upon the province.[579] The following year he published the charter and other public acts in pamphlet form.[580] In 1747 he printed in his paper the laws relating to ministers, teachers, churches and schools.[581] He also printed the acts of the Provincial Assembly when-

---

[574] S 3-1-49.
[575] S 222.
[576] Chapter I.
[577] GP 3, 10.
[578] See Chapter I.
[579] S 37 ff.
[580] S 48.
[581] S 84, 85.

ever he considered them to be of direct interest to his readers.[582] In 1765 Miller was authorized by the Assembly to publish in German the resolutions it had passed against the Stamp Act.[583] After the war all the German papers reported the doings of the State Legislature, as well as those of the National Congress. The Legislature ordered[584] its journal to be printed in both English and German, beginning with 1786.

Although the Mennonites and Dunkers were generally opposed to participation in politics and governmental affairs, yet Saur was continually urging his readers to exercise their right of suffrage. In 1748 he urged all to vote, including those "im Busch" (backwoods) even if they did not receive special notice.[585] In 1755 he enumerated[586] the advantages of becoming naturalized as follows: the Germans would then have the same freedom of buying and selling as the English, their transfers of real estate would be more secure than before, and they could vote. In the next issue he published the qualifications necessary for naturalization.[587] The second Saur republished these qualifications and also enumerated the advantages of citizenship.[588]

Despite the attempts to make intelligent voters of the

[582] See S 155.
[583] M 196.
[584] PC 251; GZ 27.
[585] S 100.
[586] S 178.
[587] S 4-1-55. These were (1) seven years' residence in the province, although the applicant was permitted to be absent for two years; (2) taking of the Lord's Supper within twelve weeks before the date of naturalization; (3) taking an oath or affirmation of allegiance. Persons of the Catholic faith were disqualified.
[588] S 7-20-59. Miller likewise urged the Germans to become nauturalized (M 138).

Germans, signs are not lacking that the attempts were not completely successful. In a communication to Bache's *General Advertiser* which later appeared in the *Philadelphische Correspondenz*, the writer said that, while the Germans were industrious and economical, it was immaterial to them to whom the reins of government were entrusted.[589] In an article in the Reading *Adler* the complaint was made that the Germans were easily misled in politics and handed in, on election day, ballots containing the names of those for whom they did not intend to vote.[590]

The advisability of military preparedness was one of the big questions throughout the eighteenth century. The Dunker Saurs, as we have seen,[591] were opposed to all war. Other editors also attacked military preparations in times of peace. The *Neue Unpartheyische Lancäster Zeitung* contained a letter[592] attacking the new Pennsylvania militia law of 1788 for various reasons, among which are the following: it compelled the men to abandon farming, it brought the youth into bad company, it made women and children lazy,[593] it gave rise to a system of oppression and it nourished the spirit of war, which is always unfavorable to the arts of peace. In 1793 the Reading paper quoted[594] Doctor Johnson on the horrors of war and on the folly of people who enter upon war lightheartedly. When a bill was introduced in 1798 into the Pennsylvania House of Representatives to forbid the government from going to

---

[589] PC, 227.

[590] A 28 This statement must be somewhat discounted, because it was published during the political controversy between Federalists and Antifederalists.

[591] Chapters I and II.

[592] NUL 54.

[593] Reference to the holidays on inspection days.

[594] NUR 223.

war unless the country was attacked, seven Germans voted for the bill and five against it, although it was defeated by a vote of thirty-seven to thirty-three.[595] The one German newspaper article in favor of a standing army was written by C. C. Reiche for his *Postbothe*. He declared[596] that the only argument against a standing army was the danger of usurpation of power, but that this danger could easily be avoided if the people did not entrust too much power into the hands of the army leaders. Reiche then proceeded to enumerate the advantages of such an army. It was more reliable for protecting the country from foreign attack than the militia, which was worthless without the example of a long-drilled standing army. Moreover, such an army was a good place for wild young men, since it developed them into useful citizens.

It is exceedingly interesting to trace in the newspapers the attitude which the Pennsylvania Germans took toward the various events and public questions of the last half of the eighteenth century and to see how they tried to act in accordance with their ideas of liberty. During the French and Indian War the Germans who were under the leadership of Saur were opposed to the war, because they felt that the Indians could easily have been placated if the white men had made a serious attempt to do so. Ten years before the war really started Saur had said that it was no wonder that the Indians allied themselves with the French against the so-called Christians of Pennsylvania.[597] Because the Quakers, assisted by the non-resistant German sectarians, were very strong in the Provincial Assembly, the

[595] DP 13. Naturally the Federalists were opposed to the bill and the Antifederalists supported it.
[596] GP 12.
[597] S 45.

preparations for war were undoubtedly very much retarded. In 1755 when Saur was accused of having accepted money as a reward for using his influence to elect Quakers to the Assembly, he replied that the accusation was a falsehood; he had written letters to Germany on his arrival in America, praising the country because it was so free; but now people wanted to make it militaristic; he was opposed to this attempt and would again urge his readers to vote for Quakers.[598] After the king had vetoed the long delayed militia bill[599] of 1755, Saur sarcastically said that the cause of the veto lay in the fact that discipline under the bill's provisions would be too lax and that only good people could be accepted into the militia.[600] In the fight between the governor and the Assembly concerning the new militia bill, Saur refrained from making any comments, simply reporting the facts.[601] He was always prepared to lend his influence to any attempt to make peace with the Indians. In 1756 he reported that the Quakers and the peaceful Germans were willing to contribute money to aid in the establishment of a permanent peace with the red men.[602] When a treaty of peace was at last concluded with the Indians east of the Susquehanna in November, 1756,[603] he was so well pleased that he published in book form an account of the conferences which led to the treaty.[604] In 1758 he attacked the government because it was too tardy in answering the claims of the Indians, saying, " Wie man hört, so kloppfen einige Indianer

---

[598] S 184.
[599] S 12–1–55.
[600] S 198.
[601] S 202, 210, 4–16–57.
[602] S 195.
[603] S 11–27–56.
[604] S 204.

aufs neue an der unrechten Thür."⁶⁰⁵ For this article he was called before General Forbes to answer the charge of printing articles unfavorable to the government. Saur defended himself by saying that he always did what he thought was for the good of the country. He was dismissed after a hearing which lasted three minutes.⁶⁰⁶

None of the Germans, however, sympathized with the French, so far as we know, and probably all of them were willing to assist the English cause in some way or other. The Pennsylvanians did their part in furnishing the ill-fated Braddock's expedition with teams and provisions. Braddock was reported to have said that the teams from Lancaster, York and Cumberland Counties were the best that had arrived and that the Pennsylvanians were doing much more for the expedition than the Marylanders and Virginians.⁶⁰⁷ It was also said that Braddock had sent a letter to his superiors praising the Pennsylvanians for so willingly helping to provide the expedition with teams, etc., in contrast with some of the other colonies.⁶⁰⁸ When somebody in Pennsylvania wrote to London, claiming that the Germans helped Braddock only because they were afraid that their teams would be confiscated, Saur replied that the English government knew better.⁶⁰⁹ In 1755 he showed more restraint about printing news than many of our modern papers do in war time. He refused⁶¹⁰ to publish an account of an article which bitterly attacked the Germans, because he feared that it would engender ill-feeling between the German and the English colonists at a

⁶⁰⁵ S 6-24-58.
⁶⁰⁶ S 219.
⁶⁰⁷ S 181.
⁶⁰⁸ S 11-1-55.
⁶⁰⁹ S 189.
⁶¹⁰ S 184.

time when harmony was essential for the success of the Braddock expedition.

When the Indians began to attack the outlying settlements in Pennsylvania, like Gnadenhütten,[611] the Germans on the frontier organized companies[612] in order to guard the passes of the Blue Ridge Mountains.[613] One of these so-called "watch companies" was composed of twenty-five German settlers from Berks and Northampton Counties, who were kept on the frontier in active service for thirty-nine days. The cost[614] of keeping the company in the field was paid by the inhabitants of several townships on the border.[615] Many colonists of German descent also enlisted in the militia. Thus, one of the first companies organized under the militia law of 1755 was composed of unmarried Germans from Rockhill Township (probably Bucks County) with Jacob Arndt as captain, Anton Müller as lieutenant and Nicolaus Conrad as corporal.[616] This company was ordered shortly after being enrolled to proceed to Gnadenhütten, in the vicinity of which we find it stationed in the month of April, 1756.[617] In the same year the king gave permission to raise a regiment of soldiers which was to be commanded by German, Swiss and Dutch Protestants.[618] This "Royal American Regiment," as it was called, was composed chiefly of Pennsylvania Germans.

One of the most prominent Germans of Pennsylvania prior to 1760 was Conrad Weiser, the famous Indian in-

---

[611] See Chapter II.
[612] The frontier people of other nationalities did the same.
[613] S 187.
[614] 104 pounds 11 sh. 4 d.
[615] S 12-25-56.
[616] S 188.
[617] S 5-1-56.
[618] S 8-1-56.

terpreter. His inestimable services in bringing the white men and the Indians to a better mutual understanding are not discussed directly in the newspapers, but his name is frequently mentioned. Two instances will serve to illustrate how well he understood the red men and how highly they esteemed him. In 1747[619] Saur's paper contained a long article by Weiser on the religion of the Indians, the material for which he had collected during his journeys among them. In 1769,[620] several years after Weiser's death, the only son of a powerful old Iroquois chief, Seneca George, was murdered near Shamokin by a member of a hunting party. The nephew of Conrad Weiser was suspected of the crime and was arrested. When the representatives of the colony met the old chief, Conrad Weiser's son told him who the suspected murderer was, and assured him that the Weiser family would do all in its power to have the slayer brought to justice. Then Seneca George, although greatly grieved at the loss of his son, declared himself satisfied and burst into a panegyric over Conrad Weiser, his dear friend of former days.

On the passing of the Stamp Act by the British Parliament, the struggle between the colonies and the mother country began to assume large proportions. In this struggle the Germans, like the other colonists, were divided in their sympathies although there is hardly any doubt that the majority of them favored the colonies. The one newspaper of the period of which I have located an almost complete file, Miller's *Staatsbote*, always opposed England. Its views are so similar to those expressed by the Anglo-American press that it is often impossible to decide whether the articles on contemporary events were original ones or

[619] S 78.
[620] M 391, 400.

were copied from other newspapers.[621] In the *Staatsbote* of August 20, 1764, Miller urged all the colonies to follow the example of Rhode Island, which had appointed a committee to confer with similar committees from other colonies concerning the formulation of plans for preventing the passing of the Stamp Act by the House of Commons and for securing the repeal of the Navigation Laws. The first news of the passing of the Stamp Act was contained in the issue of April 15, 1765. When Miller announced[622] that the act was to go into effect on November 1, 1765, he added, "The great Lisbon earthquake occurred on All Saints' Day." After this announcement he attacked the act frequently in his paper.[623] On the arrival of the stamped paper, he inserted[624] the following at the top of the first column of the first page.

America, o du durch ein allzu frühes Urtheil zur Sclaverey verdammtes America!—ist es denn deine Treue,—dein kindliches Gehorsam,—deine erschöpften Schätze,—und die Blutsströhme die deine Söhne vergossen haben zur Ausbreitung des Ruhms der Brittischen Waffen, sind diese es, sage ich, welche das Land das ja deine Mutter ist gereizet haben so unrechtmäszig dich anstatt sanfter Windeln in Jammer einzuwickeln, durch Entreissung der allerliebsten Vorrechte deiner Kinder—oder hat die Untreue es gethan?—aber, ach! die Worte fehlen mir,—und die ängstlichen und schmerzlichen Zähren halten meine Feder auf,—O mein Vaterland, mein Vaterland!

On October 28, 1765, he notified his readers that he would suspend the publication of the paper until he could

---

[621] This similarity of viewpoint may be considered as another indication that the English and German elements were rapidly being transformed into a new nationality.
[622] M 177.
[623] M 184, 185, 191.
[624] M 195.

discover a way to break the chains forged for the American people and to escape the unendurable slavery.[625] He characterized the Stamp Act as "the most unconstitutional law which these colonies could ever have imagined." In the lower right-hand corner of the first page, he printed, like the other papers, a skull and cross bones with the caption, "Dis ist der Platz für den Todespein erregender Stämpel." Three days later he published an extra as a farewell present ("Abschieds-Geschenk"). On November 18 the *Staatsbote* reappeared on unstamped paper. The next year when the news of the repeal of the Stamp Act arrived, Miller published the news joyfully and gratefully.[626]

Saur's paper presumably opposed the Stamp Act also. We find that Miller attacked[627] Saur bitterly because the latter declared in Number 347 of his paper that his (Saur's) pamphlet on the Stamp Act had influenced the Pennsylvania Assembly to pass the resolutions about the Act. In this pamphlet Saur favored a convention to petition the king for the repeal of the Act. Miller also accused a German editor of declaring that many of the latter's friends favored the odious legislation.[628] If the German editor was Saur, it might seem to indicate that he was not as strongly opposed to it as Miller.

The anniversary of the repeal of the Stamp Act was celebrated by the colonists up to the days of the Revolution. Thus we are told that on March 18, 1775, a large number of German Protestants gathered at the house of

[625] This is exactly what the English language papers of Philadelphia did.
[626] M 227, 228.
[627] M 196.
[628] M 199.

David Grim in New York and celebrated the anniversary of the repeal of the Stamp Act with the usual simplicity and solemnity.[629]

The momentous events between the repeal of the Stamp Act and the battles of Lexington and Concord were duly recorded by Miller, who always emphasized the injustice of England. Thus when legal proceedings were instituted in 1771 by the Royal government of Massachusetts against Isaiah Thomas, publisher of the "Massachusetts Spy," Miller expressed his sympathy for him.[630] Triumphantly he told about the reception of the taxed tea at the various places in 1773.[631] After the closing of the port of Boston, he gave accounts of the meetings held in the different Pennsylvania counties for the purpose of deciding what action should be taken. The committees which signed the resolutions agreed upon in the counties of Philadelphia,[632] Northampton,[633] Berks,[634] Lancaster[632] and York[635] contained members with German names. There were also many Germans among the Pennsylvania deputies who met at Philadelphia on July 15, 1774, as for instance Ludwig, Bärtsch and Schlosser of Philadelphia, Schlauch of Lancaster County, Schultz of Berks County, Küchlein and Arndt of Northampton County.[636] When the Continental Congress convened, the *Staatsbote* published long accounts of its acts and proceedings.

Many Pennsylvania Germans participated actively in

[629] M 689.
[630] M 515 ff.
[631] M 623.
[632] M 649.
[633] M 650.
[634] M 651.
[635] M 652.
[636] M 653.

the War for Independence. Before June, 1775, four companies of infantry had been organized in Reading. One of them, known as the "Company of Old Men," was composed of eighty High Germans, more than forty years of age. Many of them had seen military service in Europe; the leader was ninety-seven years old and had been in seventeen engagements during his forty years of military service. The company wore black ribbons on their hats in order to symbolize their sorrow over the lamentable events which had compelled them to take up arms for the preservation of that liberty which they had obtained by coming to this country.[637] In the same year a German fusileer company of one hundred and seventy-two men was raised in South Carolina.[638] Pulasky recruited his corps chiefly in the vicinity of Bethlehem. *Das Pennsylvanische Zeitungsblat* contained[639] eight stanzas of doggerel on "Pulasky's Chor."[640]

Miller's *Staatsbote* was the great German champion of the struggling colonists up to the time of this journal's final discontinuance in 1779. In fact, it is probable that one of the reasons for the loyalty of many of the Germans to the colonists' cause was the contagious enthusiasm with which this paper preached the justice of the Revolution. Through the darkest days of the war Miller never wavered in his faith as to the ultimate outcome. It seems most fitting that this sturdy upholder of liberty should have had the honor of being the first editor to announce in his paper

[637] M 699.
[638] M 713.
[639] Ba 19.
[640] One famous Pennsylvania German general must be mentioned here, Peter Mühlenberg, the son of the Lutheran patriarch, H. M. Mühlenberg. At the beginning of the war he was a minister in Virginia, but he entered on active military service rising to the rank of general.

the Declaration of Independence. In the issue of Friday, July 5, 1776, the following notice appeared, "Gestern hat der Achtbare Congresz dieses Vesten Landes die Vereinigten Colonien Freye und Unabhängige Staaten erkläret." In the next issue, on July 9, he published the complete text of the Declaration in German.

Just as among other nationalities, we find among the Germans also many who were lukewarm and even inimical to the war. Of course, all of the Dunkers and Mennonites who adhered completely to the doctrine of non-resistance were opposed to the war, although they may have been entirely convinced about the justice of the patriots' contentions. Since they refused to bear arms, they were compelled to pay extra taxes.[641] However, there was probably a small minority of Germans who sympathized with England. We have seen that the sons of Christoph Saur, the second, continued the old paper under the name of *Der Pennsylvanische Staats-Courier* as a Tory organ during the British occupation of Philadelphia. The issue of February 18, 1778, contained[642] a bitter attack on the patriots. The article declared that if in a country bankrupt merchants became state councillors and a dismissed postmaster an ambassador to a royal court, the outlook for the State was dangerous and that, if the ministers of religion became political market criers and prescribed quack remedies for the State, the evils united and increased. Since this was the case, the editors gave a prescription which began as follows, "A sufficient weight of lead, make it into pills, add the usual amount of genuine gunpowder to each, distribute them in equal shares among twenty thousand fine soldiers in addition to the proper small mili-

[641] M 763.
[642] Ba 17.

tary syringes for application. Aim your instrument so that they hit the part of the patient in which most of the bad sap has been collected," etc. To this, *Das Pennsylvanische Zeitungsblat* answered that such a cure might be effective for people who had a phlegmatic temperament and who were really as sick as the Saurs pretended; but it was dangerous to try it upon strong, healthy and choleric people, because they might pour into the doctors' faces the prescribed pills and powder.

The Saur Tory paper could not posibly have had much influence because most of the Germans were living in the territory under the control of the patriots, who certainly did not allow the sheet to circulate, and because it was so coarse and devoid of fairness that it could not convert any reasonable man to its doctrines. There were, however, other Germans in the colonies, besides the Saurs, who were active in the British cause. For instance, in 1778 two Germans of Lancaster County, Münzing and Mayer, were hanged as spies in the city of Lancaster.[643]

The Germans took an active part in the reconstruction work after the war. When the Federal Convention was holding its sessions in Philadelphia in 1787, the *Neue Unpartheyische Lancäster Zeitung* and the *Philadelphische Correspondenz* urged their readers to support it. The former published[644] an "Ermunterungslied zur Eintracht an die Bürger der Vereinigten Staaten, bey Gelegenheit der in Philadelphia versammelten Convention," which concluded as follows:

> Demuth bleibe unser Ruhm,
> Freyheit unser Eigenthum,

[643] Ba 7.
[644] NUL 1.

> Sucht nur in der Freyheit Ehre!
> Demnach, werthe Deutsche Brüder,
> Hand in Hand, ihr Bürgerglieder,
> Singt und unsrer Leider Schall
> Sey der Blauenberge Hall!
> Hallet täglich unsere Lieder
> Auch von Staat zu Staate wieder!
> Wer von deutscher Treue glüht,
> Singe immer dieses Lied.

In the next number of the paper,[645] we find a full column article giving arguments in favor of a centralized federal government, and on September 26 the paper contained a translation of the entire text of the Constitution. When the State Assembly passed a law by a vote of forty-three to nineteen to call a convention for consideration of the proposed constitution, the editor pointed with pleasure to the fact that twelve Germans of both parties were among the majority, while only one was included in the opposition.[646] The *Philadelphische Correspondenz* published many communications for and against the constitution, although the editor favored it.[647]

When the State convention of Pennsylvania met in November of that year, Friedrich Augustus Mühlenberg, a brother of General Peter Mühlenberg, was chosen president of the convention.[648] After the news of the ratification of the constitution by the convention had arrived at Lancaster, the inhabitants organized a big celebration.[649] While the citizens of German descent were apparently well pleased with the constitution, those of other nationalities were sometimes not so well disposed toward it, as may be

---

[645] NUL 2.
[646] NUL 10, 12.
[647] PC 335 ff.
[648] NUL 17.
[649] NUL 21.

seen from the riots which occurred in Carlisle, when the attempt was made to celebrate the ratification.[650] After the acceptance of the constitution by the required number of States, Philadelphia celebrated the event with an imposing parade, in which the publishers of the *Correspondenz* took part and distributed a German ode, specially written for the occasion.[651]

The Pennsylvania Germans were justly proud because one of their number, Friedrich A. Mühlenberg, had the honor to be elected the Speaker of the first national House of Representatives.[652] In a long communication in the *Philadelphische Correspondenz* an anonymous writer expressed[653] his satisfaction with this fact in the following terms:

> This thought stirred me deeply that a German possessed merit enough to be considered worthy by the biggest, best and wisest men whom America could produce and who were called together for the loftiest purpose, worthy of presiding at their deliberations, on which the weal and woe of millions of human beings depend.
>
> The blood of the grandchildren of our grandchildren will proudly well up in their hearts when they will read in the histories of America that the first speaker in the House of Representatives of the United States of America under the new constitution was a German, born of German parents in Pennsylvania.

Mühlenberg was also Speaker of the third House.[654]

In General Saint Clair's ill-starred expedition against the Indians of the Ohio Valley in 1791, there were a considerable number of soldiers from Lancaster and Berks

[650] NUL 24, 25.
[651] PC 375, 376, 377.
[652] NUR 8.
[653] PC₂ 37.
[654] PC₂ 255.

Counties.[655] The militia of Lancaster likewise accompanied General Wayne to suppress the Whiskey Rebellion in western Pennsylvania.[656]

The Germans in America, always interested in the cause of human liberty, at first warmly greeted the French Revolution. The Lancaster German paper printed in full the French Constitution of 1791.[657] On May 18, 1793, the German Republican Society of Philadelphia sent a committee to Citizen Genet of the French Republic and presented him with a written address, declaring that they were in the fullest accord with his principles and that they saw with pain and disgust the alliance of all European autocrats against liberty, and their united endeavors to put a check upon the popular will of France.[658] This enthusiasm for France was somewhat cooled when the news of the excesses of 1793 reached this country, so that the German voters of Pennsylvania gradually came to be sharply divided between the Federalists and the Antifederalists, between the party favoring England and the one favoring France. If the French Reign of Terror in addition to the attack on Christianity had not shocked the piety of the Pennsylvania Germans, it is probable that almost all of them would have supported the Antifederalists.

Since the Germans were thus divided, their newspapers took part in the terribly bitter political campaigns of 1798–1800, attacking each other with the same venom and vulgarity displayed by the Anglo-American press. The first direct political attack which I have discovered in a German paper was published in the *Readinger Zeitung* of October

---

[655] NUR 150.
[656] PC_2 344.
[657] NUL 226, 227, 228, 229.
[658] PC_2 212.

21, 1795. In this attack a writer signing himself "Pacificator" warned the readers against a group of people who called themselves Democrats but whom he called Jacobins.

These people have indeed been a great help in shaking off the yoke of England but they are turbulent individuals, who do not want to be subservient to any government, not even to the laws made by themselves. They desire confusion always.

About a month later two answers to this attack were published in the paper.[659] When "Pacificator" began to make his rebuttal,[660] the editor of the paper called[661] the attention of his readers to these articles, advising them to preserve the papers in order that they could refer to them in the dangerous times that seemed to be approaching.

Before many more months had elapsed, however, Jungmann, as well as the other editors, refused to print communications favoring the party to which they were opposed. Gradually the attacks on both sides increased in bitterness until they attained their climax in 1798 and 1799, the German Federalist papers imitating Cobbett's *Peter Porcupine's Gazette* and the Antifederalists using Bache's "Aurora"[662] as their model. Each side was firmly convinced of its rôle as the protector of liberty and persuaded that its opponents were trying to overthrow all the highly cherished institutions of the country. The Alien and Sedition Laws of 1798 naturally called forth the most violent attacks and denunciations. The invectives used by the papers seem almost incredible to the present generation. For instance, *Der Deutsche Porcupein* called the Antifederalists " Die Schurtzfells Majestät," " Die Schuh-

[659] NUR 353, 354.
[660] NUR 354, 355, 356.
[661] NUR 354.
[662] Later published by Duane.

flicker und Grobschmidte," "Die politischen Kannengiesser," "Der Nasenweis," "Die Bärenhäuter," "Die Hundsfütter," "Die Schlange im Busen," "Neue Miszgeburt," "Das stinkige Franzosenblut"; to this the *Lancaster Correspondent* retaliated by calling the rival paper, "Der Freyheitshasser," "Das Lancaster Stinkthier," "Der amerikanische Esel," "Der Freund der Dummheit," "Das Lügenblatt." The Federalist *Readinger Zeitung* used the terms "Bluthunde," "Blutsuckler," "Unruhstifter," "Stümpler," "Schmierer," "Dummkopf," "Nachteule," while its opponent, the *Adler,* called Jungmann, "Das kleine schwarze sogenannte unpartheyische Zeitungs-Schmiererlein, Gottlobgen, Graf Kalabast-Philosoph und Erb-Herr von Schimpf Hansen."[663]

During these troublous political times, there also occurred the one serious Pennsylvania German rebellion against State authority. In 1798 the national government passed a law whereby all houses were to be taxed on the basis of the number and size of the windows which each contained. This house tax law aroused determined opposition in the German Antifederalist counties of Northampton and Berks, particularly in the former. As early as January 9, 1799, *Der Deutsche Porcupein* reported that there was a probability that the militia would have to be called out in order to collect the taxes in Northampton County. Two weeks later a communication[664] was printed giving a dark picture of the state of affairs in this county. The Germans were said to be erecting numerous liberty poles, and could have easily paid their taxes with the money which they spent in drinking and shooting.

[663] A 107.
[664] The *Porcupein* copied the article from the *Pennsylvanische Correspondenz.*

Drinking French brandy made even grayhaired men swing their hats and shout, "Hurrah, hurrah! Dämm de President, dämm de Congresz, dämm de Arischdokratz!"

The unpopularity of the tax caused the inhabitants of Northampton and of the upper parts of Bucks and Montgomery to resist the assessors. When the United States marshal arrested some of these objectors, a crowd under the leadership of John Fries, a German auctioneer and captain of the militia, surrounded the inn at Bethlehem in which the marshal was guarding his prisoners and compelled him to release them.[665] Then events began to move rapidly. President Adams issued a proclamation requesting the disturbers of the peace to return to their homes.[666] The militia of Pennsylvania and the neighboring States was called out, although the Antifederalists introduced a resolution into the Pennsylvania House of Representatives to refuse aid to the national government in its attempt to quell the uprising.[667] When the militia arrived in the disaffected locality, all opposition disappeared. The ringleaders, who did not deliver themselves up voluntarily, surrendered when they saw the military force. Fries was auctioneering when the soldiers approached. On seeing them he took to flight but was taken prisoner after a chase of two miles.[668] The prisoners, all Pennsylvania Germans, were promptly put on trial. The United States circuit court which met at Philadelphia returned a true bill against John Fries on April 23, 1799,[669] and the trial started a week later.[670] On May 9, he was found guilty of

[665] NUR 526; DP 64, A 115.
[666] NUR 527.
[667] NUR 529.
[668] DP 68.
[669] NUR 533 et al.
[670] NUR 534 et al.

high treason,[671] but was granted a new trial.[672] About a year later he was given this new trial and was again convicted. With two of his companions, Gettmann and Hainey (Hönig), he was sentenced to be hanged at Quakertown, Bucks County, on May 23, 1800;[673] they were, however, pardoned by President Adams.[674] Twenty-four other Germans were sentenced to fines and imprisonment. Thus ended the Fries rebellion, of which some echoes are still lingering in the localities where it occurred.

How can this rebellion of the Pennsylvania Germans be explained when we remember their reputation as law-abiding, peace-loving citizens? The explanation is probably found in their love of liberty, to which I have so often alluded. In common with many others the Germans cherished personal liberty very highly. When they heard that assessors were coming to count and measure their window panes for taxation purposes, they may have believed that the government intended to tax the light that entered their houses,—hence the sarcastic terms, "Häusermesser" and "Fensterscheibenzähler,"[675] which they applied to the assessors.[676] It must, however, be remembered that the majority of the Germans of both political parties remained loyal to the government. Almost all, if not all, of the better educated were opposed to the rebellion. Thus the Reverend Helmuth, the pastor of Zion's Lutheran Church of Philadelphia, wrote an appeal to the people of Northampton County to desist from their rebellious attitude,[677]

[671] NUR 535 et al.
[672] NUR 536.
[673] NUR 587.
[674] NUR 589.
[675] UH 2.
[676] The suspicion thus aroused was probably secretly encouraged by the Antifederalist leaders.
[677] DP 67; NUR 530.

into which they had been misled. Even that inveterate enemy of the Federalists, the Reading *Adler*, decried the use of force in the following characteristic article.[678]

Est ist gewis für jeden guten Republican eine bedauernswürdige Sache, dasz man sich in Northampton County dem Tax-Geseze des Congresses widersezt hat. So lang ein Geseze besteht, musz jeder brave Bürger demselben sich unterwerfen. Es giebt kein erlaubtes Mittel sich einer bösen Taxe oder einem schlimmen Geseze zu entziehen, als die gesezgebende Macht durch Bittschriften dahin zu vermögen, selbige aufzuheben. Gewalt und Loszreiszungen sind nur gar zu unrechte und unkluge Wege. Diejenigen, so eine stehende Armee haben wollen, die, so eine Regierungs-Veränderung wünschen, werden sich im Herzen freuen, wenn sich das Volk denen Gesezen mit Gewalt widersezt. Denn ein solch verkehrtes Betragen zieht Klagen und Ursachen nach sich, kriegerische Hülfe auszurufen und also der Regierung die Obermacht zu geben. Freye Bürger verlieren immer dabei, wenn sie sich denen Gesezen und Taxen mit Gewalt widersezen.[679]

Although the Antifederalist newspapers condemned the outbreak, they naturally opposed the government in its legal proceedings against the ringleaders. For instance, the *Härrisburg Zeitung* of May 21, 1799, contained a fierce attack on the partisan spirit which had convicted Fries of high treason; it claimed that he had not committed high treason, as it was defined by the constitution of the United States. After President Adams had pardoned Fries, Hainey and Gettmann, the *Adler* in its own witty way attempted to make political capital out of the pardon. In a full column article it described the effect of the pardon upon the Federalists of Berks County. A certain corporal

---

[678] A 177.

[679] Despite this diplomatic and clever article, a party of soldiers seized the editor, Schneider, and proceeded to flog him. See A 121.

or sergeant of Reading declared that he did not want to serve in the militia any longer. A Reading captain refused to sign a petition for the pardon, because he had been in such great danger in the Northampton County campaign. In reply to this statement the *Adler* said,

> Of course the danger into which the young hero went was most unusually great, since not a single shot was fired during tne whole campaign and the entire march was only forty miles long. What a terrible danger this was! Verily, it was a wonder that this brave young hero did not remain dead on the field, and he has done the right thing in not signing the petition for Fries, Hainey and Gettmann; he would by his signature have washed off immediately the splendor of the mighty heroic deeds which he had performed in Northampton.

On account of the pardon a Reading Irishman threatened to return to Ireland and a country merchant damned the president.[680]

After the excitement of the Fries rebellion had subsided, the German papers of both parties asumed a calmer tone. This is all the more remarkable, because in the following year the so-called political revolution of 1800 occurred. Although the papers expressed emphatic opinions about the candidates of the opposing parties, the fierce epithets of the preceding years were usually absent. The editors probably learned from the rebellion the danger of becoming too violent in their denunciations. The death of Washington, whom all Germans revered, may have also drawn the two parties closer together by reminding them of the time, twenty years before, when all of them stood arrayed against the common foe and fought for that liberty which they now interpreted so variously. Although the Federalist papers, like the *Readinger Zeitung* and *Der*

[680] A 178.

Deutsche Porcupein, had black borders around the pages of three or four issues while the Antifederalist press had only the obituary notice framed in black, the latter vied with their opponents in praising Washington as the man to whom this country owed its liberty. For instance, the Antifederalist *Philadelphische Correspondenz* published[681] a poem on Washington's death, which contained these lines,

> Ist Er nicht mehr?
> Der gute alte Waschington:
> Gott! welch ein Schlag!
> Die Erde bebt, das rauhe Meer
> Der Traurigkeit umgibt uns.
> Er fällt dahin, der Held,
> Der oftmals auf das Feld
> Des Streits sich hat begeben,
> Der Josua, den Gott hat auserwählt,
> Dis ein freyes Land zu machen,
> Ist nicht mehr hier!

This brief discussion of their attitude on public questions shows us beyond any doubt that many of the Pennsylvania Germans appreciated fully the value and duty of an active participation in public affairs. Moreover, all of them evinced an intense love of liberty, although they disagreed on the question of what constituted liberty.

[681] PC₃ 75. This poem was signed "R."

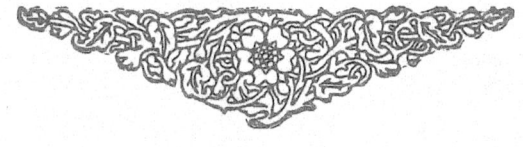

CONCLUSION.

The Pennsylvania Germans of the eighteenth century were as a class pious, charitable and honest; they loved peace and temperance; they were frugal, industrious, intelligent and progressive in their daily life; in public affairs, liberty loving and patriotic,—in a word, they possessed the qualities of nation builders in the truest sense. Admitting that they were by no means free from faults and even vices, and that development of their virtues was not only desirable but necessary, we can nevertheless confidently insist upon the claim of their sterling worth as an element of the American people.

While this conclusion is not new but mainly confirms the views of the best authorities, a new body of facts has been revealed. It may be well to enumerate some of the discoveries brought to light in my investigations. Two newspapers, of whose existence nothing was known, were found, the *Landmanns Wochenblatt* and the *Lancaster Wochenblatt*. The names of Samuel Saur's Baltimore paper of 1795–1800 and of Bärtgis' Frederick paper of 1793 were definitely ascertained. The mistake of considering the *Pennsylvanische Correspondenz* as the continuation of the *Philadelphische Correspondenz* has been corrected. A short-lived thrice-a-week edition of the latter was also discovered. Naturally much of the information about the newspapers and their editors has never appeared before.

The chapters on religion and charity probably contain

less new material than any of the others because the material was obtained to a large extent from Saur's and Miller's papers, which had been carefully studied by Seidensticker, Pennypacker, Sachse, Brumbaugh and others; however, even here many new things were found. On the other hand, the material in the chapters on education and language is to a very large extent entirely new, as, for instance, the articles by "Philoteutologos" on the German Lutheran Schools of Philadelphia and the communications to the *Philadelphische Correspondenz* on the advisability of discarding the use of the German language. Likewise much of the material of chapters six and seven had never been used before, while chapter eight contains less new material.

The bibliography of newspapers appended is, so far as I know, the only one that is approximately complete and up-to-date; in fact it is the only one that states what papers and issues are still extant and where they can be found. I may add that a complete bibliography of all Pennsylvania papers published prior to 1821 will probably appear within the next two or three years. Mr. Clarence S. Brigham of the American Antiquarian Society is preparing such a bibliography of all American newspapers prior to 1821. He has, however, not yet come to the State of Pennsylvania.

TABLE OF GERMAN AMERICAN NEWSPAPERS OF THE EIGHTEENTH CENTURY.

I have tried to make the following table of German newspapers of the eighteenth century as complete as possible. I have also included an account of the condition of the files found in the various libraries, with the date when I saw the the files. To the table, I have deemed it advisable to append a short article under the title, "Were They Ever Published?"

The following abbreviations for the various societies and libraries have been used:

A. A. S. = American Antiquarian Society, Worcester, Mass.
A. P. S. = American Philosophical Society, Philadelphia.
L. C. = Library of Congress, Washington, D. C.
P. H. S. = Historical Society of Pennsylvania, Philadelphia

NEWSPAPER INDEX.

Americanische Staatsbothe, Der. (AS)........................ 188
Chestnuthiller Wochenschrift, Die. (CW).................... 191
Deutsche Porcupein, Der. (DP)............................. 188–189
Geistliches Magazien, Ein. 179
Gemeinnützige Philadelphische Correspondenz (PC).......... 181 ff
General Post-Bothe, Der. (GP).............................. 191
General Staats-Bothe... 192
Germantauner Zeitung, Die. (GZ)........................... 186 f
Germantowner Zeitung, Die. (S)............................ 173
Härrisburg Zeitung, Die. (UH)............................. 200
Henrich Miller's Pennsylvanischer Staatsbote (M)............ 178
Hoch-Deutsche Pennsylvanische Geschicht Schreiber, Der. (S) 171
Hoch-Deutsche Pennsylvanische Journal, Das. 174
Lancaster Correspondent, Der. (H)......................... 200
Lancaster Wochenblatt, Das. 198
Lancastersche Zeitung, Die. (LZ)........................... 176
Landmanns Wochenblatt, Des. 197
Neue monatliche Readinger Magazin, Das. 199
Neue Philadelphische Correspondenz (PC₂).................. 182 ff
Neue Unpartheyische Baltimore Bote und Märyländ Staats-Register, Der. 193
Neue Unpartheyische Lancäster Zeitung (NUL).............. 188–189
Neue Unpartheyische Readinger Zeitung (NUR)............. 189–191
Neuer Unpartheyischer Eastoner Bothe...................... 192
Pennsylvanische Berichte (S)............................... 171 ff
Pennsylvanische Correspondenz, Die........................ 196
Pennsylvanische Gazette, Die............................... 181
Pennsylvanische Staats-Courier, Der........................ 180
Pennsylvanische Wochenschrift, Die........................ 196

Pennsylvanische Zeitungsblat, Das (Ba).................... 180
Philadelphier Teutsche Fama.............................. 175
Philadelphier Wochenblat, Das............................ 191
Philadelphische Correspondenz (PC₂, PC₃, PC₄)............. 181 ff and
                                                           201
Pennsylvanische Fama, Die................................ 177
Philadelphische Zeitung (1732)........................... 171
Philadelphische Zeitung (1755) (PZ)...................... 176
Philadelphisches Magazin................................. 197
Philadelphisches Staatsregister (PS)..................... 181
Unpartheyische Härrisburg Zeitung (UH)................... 199
Unpartheyische Reading Adler, Der. (A)................... 195 f
Unpartheyische York Gazette, Die......................... 194
Volksberichter, Der...................................... 201
Westliche Correspondenz, Die............................. 194
Wöchentliche Pennsylvanische Staatsbote, Der. (M)........ 177 ff
Wöchentliche Philadelphische Staatsbote, Der. (M)........ 177 ff
Name unknown (1748) Philadelphia......................... 174
Name unknown (1751) Philadelphia......................... 175
Name unknown (1786) Frederick, Maryland.................. 187
Name unknown (1786) Baltimore, Maryland.................. 187

Philadelphische Zeitung. Published by Benjamin Franklin in Philadelphia.

1732, No. 1 (May 6). Facsimile in Daniel Miller's "Early German American Newspapers" and elsewhere.
1732. No. 2 (June 24).—P.H.S. (vidimus Mar. 1917).

No more copies have been found. The paper was probably discontinued for Timothee, the editor, complains in No. 2 that he receives so little encouragement from the Germans.

Der Hoch-Deutsch Pennsylvanische Geschicht-Schreiber, Oder: Sammlung Wichtiger Nachrichten aus dem Natur- und Kirchen-Reich. Published by Christoph Saur at Germantown, at first quarterly, probably became a monthly at beginning of 1741.

In P. H. S. (Vidimus, March and April, 1917).

1739, No, 1 (Aug. 20).
1742, No. 19 (Feb. 16).
1743, Nos. 33 (Apr. 16) – 41 (Dec. 16).
1744, Nos. 42 (Jan. 16) – 53 (Dec. 16).
1745, Nos. 54 (Jan. 16) – 65 (Dec. 16). (Name changed on Oct. 16, 1745, to "Hoch-Deutsche Pennsylvanische Berichte," etc.)
1746, Nos. 66 (Jan. 16) – 77 (Dec. 16). (On and after June 16, 1746, the word, "Hoch-Deutsch" was omitted.
1747, Nos. 78 (Jan. 16) – 89 (Dec. 16).
1748, Nos. 90 (Jan. 16) – 103 (Dec. 16). (Nos. 93 and 96 are dated April 1 and June 1) Specials on first of Aug. and Oct.
1749, Nos. 104 (Jan. 16) – 115 (Dec. 16). Specials on first of March, May, June, August, Sept., Nov. and Dec.
1750, Nos. 116 (Jan. 16) – 127 (Dec. 16). Specials on first of Feb., May, June, July, Aug., Sept., Oct., and Nov.
1751, Nos. 128 (Jan. 16) – 139 (Dec. 16). Specials on first of Jan., Feb., March, April, May, June, July, Aug., Sept., Oct., Nov.
1752, Nos. 140 (Jan. 16) – 151 (Dec. 16). (Two numbers of 143.) Specials on first of Jan., Feb., March, April, May, June, July. Oct., Nov., Dec.
1753, No. 159 (Aug. 16), No. 161 (Oct. 16). Special on Aug. 1.
1754, Nos. 164 (Jan. 16) – 166 (Mar. 16).
Nos. 169 (June 16) – 171 (Aug. 16).
Nos. 174 (Nov. 16) – 175 (Dec. 16).
Specials on first of Feb., April, Aug., Sept. and Dec.
1755, No. 176 (Jan. 16).
Nos. 178 (Mar. 16) – 187 (Dec. 16).
Specials on first of Jan., Feb., March, April, May, June, July, Aug., Sept., Oct., Nov. and Dec.
1756, Nos. 188 (Jan. 16) – 195 (Aug. 16).
Nos. 196 (Sept. 18) – 199 (Dec. 11).
Specials on first of Feb., March. April, May, June, July, August. (Paper became bi-weekly on August 21 with only one issue per month numbered.) Unnumbered issues on Aug. 21, Sept. 4, Oct. 2, Oct. 30, Nov. 27, Dec. 25.
1757, Nos. 200 (Jan. 8) – 212 (Dec. 10).
Unnumbered issues every four weeks from Jan. 22 to Dec. 24.
1758, Nos. 213 (Jan. 7) – 216 (Apr. 1).
Nos. 217 (May 13) – 222 (Sept. 30).
Nos. 223 (Nov. 11) – 224 (Dec. 9).
(On Sept. 25, Saur died. After that date his son Christopher published the paper.)

Unnumbered issues every four weeks from Jan. 21 to April 15, from April 29 to Oct. 14, from Oct. 28 to Dec. 23.
1759, Nos. 225 (Jan. 5) – 227 (Mar. 2).
    Nos. 229 (May 11) – 232 (Aug. 3).
    Nos. 233 (Sept. 14) – 236 (Dec. 7).
Unnumbered issues every four weeks from Jan. 19 to Mar. 16, from Mar. 30 to Aug. 17, from Aug. 31 to Nov. 23.
1760, No. 242 (June 6), No. 244 (Aug. 1).
Unnumbered issues of Feb. 15, Feb. 29, Mar. 28, April 25, May 23.
1761, No. 249 (Jan. 2), No. 250 (Feb. 13), No. 252 (Apr. 10).
    Nos. 254 (June 5) – 255 (July 3).
    Nos. 256 (Aug. 14) – 259 (Nov. 6).
Unnumbered issues every four weeks from Mar. 27 to July 17, from July 31 to Dec. 18.
1762, No. 264 (April 9).
Unnumbered issue of Jan. 29.
1766, No. 371 (Aug. 7) (still bi-weekly).
(Title now is *Die Germantowner Zeitung*, etc., with the word "Wahrscheinlicher" for "Wichtiger.")
1775, No. 598 (Apr. 20) (still bi-weekly).
1776, No. 645 (Mar. 20) (now weekly and with the simple title of *Die Germantowner Zeitung*). Published by Christoph Saur und Sohn.
    No. 670 (Sept. 11)
1777, No. 688 (Mar. 12). (Published by Christoph Saur, jun. und Peter Saur.)
In S. W. Pennypacker's *private library* (*non vidimus*).
Dec. 16, 1743 to Nov. 16, 1745.
April, 1755, to December, 1757.
Owned by Dr. Geo. Hetrich of Birdsboro, Pa.
1777, No. 686 (Feb. 26) (vidimus, Aug. 3, 1917).
In A. P. S. (*vidimus March and September, 1917*).
1747. Nos. 84 (July 16) – 89 (Dec. 16).
1748, Nos. 90 (Jan. 16) – 103 (Dec. 16).
Supplement to No. 91. Specials on Aug. 1 and October 1.
1749, Nos. 104 (Jan. 16) – 115 (Dec. 16). Specials on first of March, May, June, Aug., Sept., Nov., and Dec.
1750, Nos. 116 (Jan. 16) – 127 (Dec. 16). Specials on first of Feb., May, June, July, Aug., Sept., Oct., Nov.
1751, Nos. 128 (Jan. 16) – 139 (Dec. 16). Specials on first of every month except Dec.

1752, Nos. 140 (Jan. 16) – 151 (Dec. 16). Specials on first of every month except Aug. and Sept.
1753, Nos. 152 (Jan. 16) – 157 (June 16).
   Nos. 159 (Aug. 16) – 162 (Nov. 16).
      Specials on the first of every month except Dec. Two copies of No. 159.

The paper probably continued up to the time when the British took Philadelphia. Christoph Saur, jun., und Peter Saur then published *Der Pennsylvanische Staats Courier* (q. v.).

Das Hoch deutsche Pennsylvanische Journal (Weekly), 1743. Published by Joseph Crellius in Philadelphia. No copies discovered.

In S 35, we learn that Joseph Crellius has started a weekly newspaper in Philadelphia and that he will use English letters until he can obtain German type. The price of the paper is ten shillings per year.

Thomas in his " History of Printing " (p. 144, Vol. II, 2d ed.) gives it the name mentioned above.

How long the paper continued we do not know, but certainly not longer than up to the spring of 1747, for Crellius has an advertisement in S 74, announcing that he intends to go to Holland next spring.

Deutsche Wöchentliche Zeitung (1748). (Name not known.) Published by Gotthart Armbrüster in Philadelphia. (No copies discovered.)

In S 95, Gotthart Armbrüster announces that he will start a weekly paper on May 27, 1748. Saur asks those people who have not paid him for his paper, not to do the same to Armbrüster.

We do not know how long its publication continued.

In Almanac of 1749 (presumably by G. Armbrüster), we read "Die Zeitung kann man haben alle 8 Tag, das Jahr vor 10 schill."

Philadelphier Teutsche Fama (1749-1750). Published by Böhm in Philadelphia. (No copies discovered.)
We do not know how often the paper was published.
The title is given in S 106.
It is mentioned in S 106, 115, 117, 119.
Since the firm Franklin and Böhm published books, it is perhaps safe to assume that this paper was also published by them. Also since Böhm died in 1751 and since Franklin probably published a bi-lingual paper during the last half of the year, we may probably conclude that this paper was the predecessor of the bi-lingual.

Deutsche und Englische Zeitung (1751) (Bi-weekly). (Name not known.) Published by Benjamin Franklin in Philadelphia. (No copies discovered.)
Seidensticker ("First Century of German Printing in America," p. 38) says:

Known only through the following advertisement in the *Pennsylvania Gazette* of Sept. 12 (1751) and later dates.
At the German Printing Office in Arch Street is now printed every Fortnight a Dutch and English Gazette, containing the freshest Advices, foreign and domestick with other entertaining and useful Matter in both Languages, adapted to the Convenience of such as incline to learn either. Subscribers to pay five Shillings per Annum.

Seidensticker doubts the statement that G. Armbrüster printed the paper,—a statement made in Thomas's "History of Printing" (2d edition, Vol. II, p. 144) and in Hildeburn's "Issues of the Press of Pennsylvania" (Vol. I, p. 265). Thomas says the name of the paper was *Die Zeitung* (Vol. II, p. 144),—a mistake probably. Without sufficient proof he identifies this paper with Armbrüster's of 1748, to which Armbrüster refers in his almanac of 1749. Although this almanac speaks of the latter paper as *Die Zeitung,* it does not follow that this was the name of the paper.

Die Lancastersche Zeitung: Oder: Ein Kurtzer Begriff der Hauptsächlichsten Ausländisch- und Einheimischen Neuigkeiten (bi-lingual) (bi-weekly). Published by H. Müller and S. Holland.

In P. H. S. (Vidimus Mar. 1917.)

1752, No. 2 (Jan. 29), No. 12 (June 16), (Beginning with No. 12 S. Holland is publisher alone.)
1752, No. 15 (July 28) – No. 16 (Aug. 11).
   No. 19 (Oct. 3).
1753, No. 31 (June 5).

I have been able to find no indication when it suspended publication.

Philadelphische Zeitung von allerhand Auswärtig- und einheimischen merck-würdigen Sachen (bi-weekly). Published by B. Franklin, General Postmeister, und Anthon Armbrüster.

In P. H. S. (Vidimus, March, 1917).

1755, No. 5 (Sept. 6), No. 11 (Nov. 27).
1756, No. 19 (Mar. 6), No. 34 (Sept. 23) No. 41 (Dec. 30).
1757, No. 42 (Jan. 14) (Two copies).
   Nos. 44 (Feb. 11) – 46 (Mar. 14).
   No. 48 (Apr. 15), No. 49 (Apr. 22), No. 50 (May 7).
   Nos. 51 (May 20) – 64 (Nov. 18).
   Nos. 67 (Dec. 17) – 68 (Dec. 31).

According to Seidensticker (op. cit., p. 49), the paper stopped with the issue of Dec. 31, 1757.

Thomas (op. cit., Vol. II, p. 147) says it was continued by Weiss and Miller, conveyancers, in 1759. It was published for them by Anthony Armbrüster about two years. In 1762 he printed it on his own account and in 1764 published it weekly on Arch St.

Die Pennsylvanische Fama (1762– ?) (weekly). Published by Anthon Armbrüster. (No copies discovered.) Mentioned only in M 34 and 35.

The publication was probably commenced in 1762 because Miller speaks of "*Fama* N. I" in M 35 and also of "N. I" and "N. II" in M 34.

Der Wöchentliche Philadelphische Staatsbote, Mit den neuesten Fremden und Einheimisch-Politischen Nachrichten: Samt den von Zeit zu Zeit in der Kirche und Gelehrten Welt sich ereignenden Merkwürdigkeiten. Published by Henrich Miller.

In the Archives of the German Society of Pennsylvania (Vidimus Dec., 1917).

1762, Nos. 1 (Jan. 18) – 50 (Dec. 27).

In the Ridgway Branch of the Philadelphia Library Company (Vidimus March, April and June, 1917).

1763, Nos. 60 (Mar. 7) – 74 (June 13).
    Nos. 79 (July 18) – 81 (Aug. 1).
    Nos. 83 (Aug. 15) – 86 (Sept. 5).
    Nos. 88 (Sept. 19) – 94 (Oct. 31).
    Nos. 98 (Nov. 28) – 102 (Dec. 26).
1764, No. 103 (Jan. 2).
    Nos. 105 (Jan. 16) – 155 (Dec. 31).
1765, Nos. 156 (Jan. 7) – 182 (July 8).
    Nos. 184 (July 22) – 198 (Oct. 28).
    No. 199 (Oct. 31) (Special farewell number before enforcement of Stamp Act).

Nos. 200 (Nov. 18) - 204 (Dec. 16).
 No. 206 (Dec. 30).
1766, Nos. 207 (Jan. 6) - 258 (Dec. 29).
1767, Nos. 259 (Jan. 5) - 310 (Dec. 28).
1768, Nos. 311 (Jan. 5) - 362 (Dec. 27).
 (Beginning with No. 311, the word "Pennsylvanische" is substituted for "Philadelphische" in the title.)
1769, Nos. 363 (Jan. 3) - 414 (Dec. 26).
1770, Nos. 415 (Jan. 2) - 460 (Nov. 13).
 Nos. 462 (Nov. 27) - 466 (Dec. 25).
1771, Nos. 467 (Jan. 1) - 519 (Dec. 31).
1772, Nos. 520 (Jan. 7) - 571 (Dec. 29).
1773, Nos. 572 (Jan. 5) - 611 (Oct. 5).
 Nos. 613 (Oct. 19) - 623 (Dec. 28.)
1774, Nos. 624 (Jan. 4) - 675 (Dec. 27).
1775, Nos. 676 (Jan. 3) - 695 (May 16).
 (Beginning with No. 696, the paper is published semi-weekly and is called "Henrich Millers Pennsylvanischer Staatsbote.")
 Nos. 696 (May 23) - 726 (Sept. 5).
 Nos. 728 (Sept. 12) - 759 (Dec. 29).
1776, Nos. 760 (Jan. 2) — 819 (July 30).
 (From No. 819, the paper appears weekly again.)
 Nos. 820 (Aug. 6) - 839 (Dec. 28).
1777, Nos. 842 (Jan. 15) - 849 (March 5).
 (Two copies of No. 844.)
 Nos. 852 (March 26) - 877 (Sept. 17).
1778, No. 878 (Aug. 5).
 Nos. 880 (Aug. 19) - 899 (Dec. 30).
 (Nos. 893-899 are mutilated.)
1779, Nos. 900 (Jan. 6) - 920 (May 26).

In L. C.

1762, No. 11 (March 29) (vidimus Feb. 1917).
1767, Nos. 259, 271 (non vidimus).
1772, Nos. 521, 538, (July 23)* 555, 557-563, 565, 569 (non vidimus).
1773, Nos. 572-587, Nos. 589-594, Nos. 597-604.
 Nos. 607-610, Nos. 613-623 (non vidimus).
1774, Nos. 624-631, Nos. 633-649, Nos. 651-656.
 Nos. 658-667 (mutilated Nos. 624 and 656) (non vidimus).
1776, No. 814 (mutilated) (non vidimus).
1777, No. 859 (mutilated) (non vidimus).

* According to Ingram's Check List; the date is apparently a mistake, since no paper was published on this date.

German American Newspapers. 179

    In P. H. S. (Vidimus, March and June, 1917).

1767, Nos. 271, 279.
1768, No. 323.
1769, No. 413.
1770, Nos. 435–447, 452, 454, 455, 457–460 (No. 460 mutilated).
1771, Nos. 467–471, Nos. 475–477, 479–515 (mutilated 479, 480, 501, 502).
1772, Nos. 520, 521 (two copies mutilated), 522, 523, 525 (mutilated), 526 (mutilated), 533–540, 542–553, 555–565, 567–571 (No. 545, two copies; No. 553 mutilated).
1773, Nos. 572–623.
1774, Nos. 624–669; Nos. 671–675.
1775, Nos. 676–752, 754–759 (No. 678, two copies; No. 716, two copies).
1776, Nos. 760–761, Nos. 753–839.
1777, Nos. 840–872 (two copies each of Nos. 853 and 869).
1778, Nos. 878–881, Nos. 883–899.
1779, Nos. 900–909, Nos. 911–915.

In the Possession of Dr. Wm. J. Campbell, Philadelphia on Sept. 18, 1917 (Vidimus).

1778, No. 879 (Aug 12).

The paper suspended publication on May 26, 1779.

Ein Geistliches Magazien. Oder: Aus den Schätzen der Schrifftgelehrten zum Himmelreich gelehrt, dargereichtes Altes und Neues. Published by Christoph Saur.

    In P. H. S. (Vidimus April and September, 1917).

1764, Vol. I Nos. 1–50.

    In Philadelphia Library Company (Locust Street branch) (Vidimus September 18, 1917).

1764, Vol. I Nos. 2–14, 20, 24–32, 47. Two copies of Nos. 7, 8, 9, 11, 14, 25, 26, 29.
1770, Vol. II Nos. 1 (with Vorrede) 3, 13, 15, Two copies of No. 1.

In the Possession of Dr. Wm. J. Campbell of Philadelphia on September 18, 1917 (Non Vidimus).

An almost complete file of Volume I.

    In State Library at Harrisburg, Pa. (Non Vidimus).

1764, Vol. I Nos. 1–50.

1770, Vol. II Nos. 1–13, 15 (No. 14 was evidently omitted because the pagination of volume is complete).

This magazine was published at irregular intervals between 1764 and 1774 and was distributed gratis.

Der Pennsylvanische Staats Courier, oder einlaufende Wöchentliche Nachrichten. Diese Zeitung wird alle Wochen herausgegeben von Christoph Saur, Jr., und Peter Saur in der Zweyten Strasze. (No copies discovered.)

1778, No. 745 (May 6). (This is a reprint appearing in Schlözer's Briefwechsel, Vol. 3, pp. 260–267.)

The number (745) would seem to indicate that this paper is simply a continuation of *Die Germantowner Zeitung*, the last number of which, seen by me, bears the date of March 12, 1777, and is numbered 688.

The paper is mentioned in Ba 5, 17, M 901.

It suspended publication when the British evacuated Philadelphia in 1778.

Das Pennsylvanische Zeitungsblat. Oder: Sammlung Sowohl Auswärtig-als Einheimischer Neuigkeiten. Published by Frantz Bailey in Lancaster.

In P. H. S. (Vidimus, June, 1917).

1778. Nos. 1 (Feb. 4) – 21 (June 24). (Complete file.)

In L. C. (Non Vidimus).

1778, Nos. 13–18, 21 (No. 18 mutilated).

The last number appeared on June 24, 1778.

Die Pennsylvanische Gazette oder der allgemeine Americanische Zeitungs-Schreiber. Published by John Dunlap, Philadelphia.

In L. C. (Vidimus, Feb. 1917).
1779, No. 1 (Feb. 3) (two copies).

In P. H. S. (Vidimus, March 1917).
1779, No. 1 (Feb. 3) (mutilated).

This paper had a very brief existence, for in PS 1 (July 21, 1779), the publishers say that there is no other German paper in the country.

Philadelphisches Staatsregister, enthaltend die neuesten Nachrichten von den merkwürdigsten In- und Ausländischen Kriegs- und Friedens-Begebenheiten; nebst verschiedenen andern gemeinnützigen Anzeigen. Published by Steiner und Cist.

In A. P. S. Philadelphia, Pa. (Vidimus, July, 1917).
1779, No. 1 (July 21), No. 2 (July 28) No. 3 (Aug. 4).
1780, No. 29 (May 24).

In New York Public Library.
1780, No. 26, (May 3) (non vidimus). (Nos. 26 and 29 have the simple title "Philadelphisches Staatsregister.")

Since Steiner was the publisher of PC which started in May, 1781, we may be confident that this paper stopped before that time.

Gemeinnützige Philadelphische Correspondenz. Melchior Steiner, publisher.

In P. H. S. (Vidimus, June, July, September, 1917).

1781, Nos. 12 (July 18) – 35 (Dec. 26).
1782, Nos. 36 (Jan. 2) – 88 (Dec. 31).
1783, Nos. 89 (Jan. 7) – 93 (Feb. 4).
    Nos. 109 (May 27) – 122 (Aug. 26).
    Nos. 124 (Sept. 9) – 129 (Oct. 14).
    Nos. 131 (Oct. 28) – 135 (Nov. 25).
    Nos. 137 (Dec. 9) – 140 (Dec. 30).
1784, Nos. 141 (Jan. 6) – 162 (June 1).
    Nos. 164 (June 15) – 168 (July 13).
    No. 179 (Sept. 28), Nos. 182 (Oct. 19) – 184 (Nov. 2).
    No. 186 (Nov. 16), No. 190 (Dec. 14).
1786, Nos. 246 (Jan. 10) – 250 (Feb. 7).
    No. 252 (Feb. 21).
    Nos. 258 (Apr. 4) – 261 (Apr. 25).
    Nos. 265 (May 23) and 277 (Aug. 15).
    Nos. 280 (Sept. 5) – 296 (Dec. 26).
1787, Nos. 298 (Jan. 9) – 307 (Mar. 13).
    Nos. 312 (Apr. 17) – 322 (June 26).
    Nos. 325 (July 17) – 326 (July 24).
    Nos. 328 (Aug. 7) – 343 (Nov. 20).
    Nos. 345 (Dec. 4) – 348 (Dec. 24).
1788, Nos. 349 (Jan. 1) – 357 (Feb. 26).
    Nos. 359 (Mar. 11) – 364 (Apr. 15).
    Nos. 369 (May 20) – 372 (June 10).
    Nos. 374 (June 24) – 388 (Sept. 30.)
    Nos. 390 (Oct. 14) – 391 (Oct. 21).
    Nos. 393 (Nov. 4) – 399 (Dec. 16).
1789, Nos. 402 (Jan. 6) – 407 (Feb. 10).
    Nos. 422 (May 26), 426 (June 23).
    Nos. 437 (Sept. 1, mutilated), 438 (Sept. 8).
    Nos. 444 (Oct. 20), 453 (Dec. 22).
1790, Nos. 476 (June 1), 486 (Aug. 10).
    From October 1, 1790, the paper appeared semi-weekly under the name of *Neue Philadelphische Correspondenz.*
1790, Nos. 2 (Oct. 5) – 27 (Dec. 31).
1791, Nos. 28 (Jan. 4) – 34 (Jan. 25).
    Nos. 38 (Feb. 8) – 130 (Dec. 30).
1792, Nos. 131 (Jan. 3) – 140 (Feb. 3).
    Nos. 145 (Feb. 28) – 150 (Mar. 30).
    (From Feb. 10, usually only one No. per week appeared, but the formal announcement of the change to a weekly was made in No. 158.)

Nos. 155 (May 1).
Nos. 157 (May 15) – 189 (Dec. 24). (With No. 182 the firm's name became Steiner and Kämmerer.) (With No. 185 the paper was called *Philadelphische Correspondenz.*)
1793, Nos. 190 (Jan. 1) – 194 (Jan. 29).
Nos. 197 (Feb. 19) – 233 (Aug. 2). (With No. 208 paper appeared semi-weekly again.)
Nos. 238 (Aug. 20) – 243 (Sept. 6). (On account of yellow fever publication was suspended between Oct. 4 and Nov. 22.)
No. 259 (Dec. 17).
1794, Nos. 270 (Jan. 24), 274 (Feb. 7), 276 (Feb. 14).
Nos. 277 (Feb. 18), 279 (Feb. 25) – 283 (Mar. 11).
Nos. 285 (Mar. 18), 288 (Mar. 28) – 290 (Apr. 4).
Nos. 293 (Apr. 15) – 295 (Apr. 25).
Nos. 298 (May 6), 301 (May 16), 303 (May 23).
No. 305 (May 30).
1795, Nos. 373 (Jan. 23), 375 (Jan. 30), 377 (Feb. 6).
Nos. 387 (Mar. 13), 395 (Apr. 14), 398 (Apr. 24).
Nos. 410 (June 5), 415 (June 23), 427 (Aug. 1).
Nos. 439 (Sept. 15), 469 (Dec. 29).
1796, Nos. 470 (Jan. 1), 475 (Jan. 19), 493 (Mar. 22).
Nos. 502 (Apr. 22), 515 (June 7), 519 (June 21).
Nos. 521 (June 28), 522 (July 1), 526 (July 15).
No. 550 (Oct. 1).

In New Series (Published by Henrich und Joseph R. Kämmerer, Jun.)
1798, Nos. 1 (May 1) – 19 (Sept. 4).
Nos. 21 (Sept. 18) – 28 (Dec. 25). (After Nov. 13 firm's name was Joseph R. Kämmerer und Comp.)
(On account of yellow fever, publication was suspended between Sept. 18 and Nov. 13.)
1799, Nos. 29 (Jan. 1) – 40 (Mar. 19).
Nos. 42 (Apr. 2) – 59 (July 30). (With No. 48, firm's name became Joseph R. Kämmerer und G. Helmbold.)
Nos. 61 (Aug. 13) – 71 (Dec. 10). (Publication suspended Aug. 27 – Oct. 22 on account of fever.)
Nos. 73 (Dec. 24) – 74 (Dec. 31).
1800, Nos. 75 (Jan. 7) – 79 (Feb. 4).
Nos. 83 (Mar. 7) – 85 (Mar. 21).
George Helmbold, Jr., is publisher of issues No. 83ff.
No. 87 (Apr. 4).
No. 27 (Apr. 23).
The publishers are now G. Helmbold and J. Geyer. The paper is again called *Neue P. C.* Why the new series does not start with

No. 1, I cannot say. It may be that it took the number of the *Stadt Philadelphische Correspondenz* (q. v.) which started on Tuesday, Feb. 11, and probably made its final appearance as a thrice-a-week paper on Saturday, April 5, *i.e.*, with No. 24. Then if the paper appeared every Wednesday thereafter the issue of April 23 would be No. 27. This is all the more probable because the issue of April 4 is marked as No. 754 of the old series and the issue of April 23 has No. 758. If the Saturday issue (April 5) was marked No. 755 of the old series, we will get No. 758 on April 23.

Nos. 40 (July 23) – 41 (July 30).

In A. P. S. (Vidimus, March, June, September, 1917).

1783, Nos. 129 (Oct. 14) – 136 (Dec. 2).
Nos. 138 (Dec. 16) – 139 (Dec. 23).
1784, Nos. 141 (Jan. 6) – 151 (Mar. 16).
Nos. 154 (Apr. 6) – 166 (June 29).
Nos. 169 (July 20) – 171 (Aug. 3).
Nos. 174 (Aug. 24), 175 (Aug. 31), 177 (Sept. 14).
Nos. 181 (Oct. 12) – 183 (Oct. 26).
No. 191 (Dec. 21).
1785, Nos. 205 (Mar. 29), 206 (Apr. 5).
Nos. 208 (Apr. 19) – 210 (May 3).
Nos. 212 (May 17) – 213 (May 24).
Nos. 216 (June 14) – 217 (June 21).
Nos. 219 (July 5) – 223 (Aug. 2).
Nos. 225 (Aug. 16), 227 (Aug. 30), 228 (Sept. 6).
No. 234 (Oct. 18).
Nos. 237 (Nov. 8) – 239 (Nov. 22).
Nos. 242 (Dec. 13), 244 (Dec. 27).
1786, Nos. 245 (Jan. 3), 247 (Jan. 17), 248 (Jan. 24).
Nos. 250 (Feb. 7), 251 (Feb. 14), 255 (Mar. 14).
Nos. 264 (May 16), 267 (June 6) – 271 (July 4).
Nos. 274 (July 25), 277 (Aug. 15), 278 (Aug. 22).
Nos. 281 (Sept. 12), 282 (Sept. 19).
Nos. 289 (Nov. 7) – 292 (Nov. 28).
No. 295 (Dec. 19).
1787, Nos. 297 (Jan. 2), 302 (Feb. 6).

In State Library at Harrisburg, Pa. ((Vidimus, July, 1917).

1791, Nos. 30 (Jan. 11) – 130 (Dec. 30).
1792, Nos. 131 (Jan. 3) – 189 (Dec. 24).
1793, Nos. 190 (Jan. 1) – 250 (Oct. 1).
Nos. 252 (Nov. 22) – 263 (Dec. 31).

1794, Nos. 264 (Jan. 3) –366 (Dec. 30).
1795, Nos. 367 (Jan. 2) – 464 (Dec. 11) (No. 367 mutilated).
    Nos. 466 (Dec. 18) – 469 (Dec. 29).
1796, Nos. 470 (Jan. 1) – 472 (Jan. 8).
    No. 475 (Jan. 19).
    Nos. 477 (Jan. 26) – 484 (Feb. 19).
    Nos. 486 (Feb. 26) – 501 (Apr. 19).
    Nos. 503 (Apr. 26) – 519 (June 21).
    No. 521 (June 28).
    Nos. 523 (July 5) – 574 (Dec. 30).

In L. C. (*Non Vidimus*).

1781, No. 29 (Nov. 14).
1783, No. 137 (Dec. 9).
1787, Nos. 307 (Mar. 13), 314 (May 1), 319 (June 5, mutilated).
1790, Nos.   July 3,* No. 6 (Oct. 19).
1794, Nos. 282 (Mar. 7), 285 (Mar. 18).
1795, No. 398 (Apr. 24).
1796, No. 530 (July 29).

In Private Library of Rev. Wm. J. Hinke, Auburn, New York (*Vidimus, Oct. 24, 1917*).

1790, No. 457 (Jan. 19), No. 21 (Dec. 10).
1791, No. 63 (May 10), No. 95 (Aug. 30).
1792, No. 158 (May 22).
1794, No. 265 (Jan. 7), No. 267 (Jan. 14).
    No. 273 (Feb. 4), No. 311 (June 20).
1800, No. 29 (May 7).

In Harvard College Library (*Vidimus, October, 1917*).

1785, Nos. 193 (Jan. 4) – 226 (Aug. 23).
    No. 229 (Sept. 13).
1786, Nos. 287 (Oct. 24), 288 (Oct. 31).
1791, No. 120 (Nov. 25).
1795, No. 437 (Sept. 8).
    Nos. 441 (Sept. 22) – 449 (Oct. 20).
    Nos. 450 (Oct. 27) – 455 (Nov. 10).
1796, Nos. 485 (Feb. 23), 490 (Mar. 11).
    Nos. 561 (Nov. 15), 570 (Dec. 16).
1797, No. 585 (Feb. 7).

In A. A. S. (*Vidimus, October, 1917*).

1794, Nos. 314 (July 1), 319 (July 18).

*According to Ingram's Check List; the date is probably a misprint.

1796, Nos. 502 (April 22) – 504 (April 29).

In Krauth Memorial Library, Lutheran Theological Seminary, Philadelphia (Vidimus, Sept. 1918).

1781, Nos. 14 (Aug. 1), 18 (Aug. 29).
1782, No. 59 (June 12).
1783, Nos. 90 (Jan. 14), 91 (Jan. 21).
1786, Nos. 253 (Feb. 28), 254 (Mar. 7).
1789, Nos. 435 (Aug. 18), 443 (Oct. 13).
1792, No. 143 (Feb. 17).
1794, Nos. 277 (Feb. 18), 328 (Aug. 19).

Die Germantauner Zeitung (bi-weekly). Published by Leibert and Billmeyer.

In P. H. S. (Vidimus Sept., 1917).

1785, Nos. 2 (Feb. 22) – 9 (May 31).
　　　Nos. 12 (July 12) – 14 (Aug. 9).
　　　No. 16 (Sept. 6).
　　　Nos. 22 (Nov. 29) – 23 (Dec. 13).
1786, Nos. 25 (Jan. 10) – 27 (Feb. 7).
　　　Nos. 30 (Mar. 21), 32 (Apr. 18).
　　　Nos. 40 (Aug. 8) – 43 (Sept. 19).
　　　Nos. 45 (Oct. 17) – 50 (Dec. 26).
1787, Nos. 51 (Jan. 9) – 69 (Sept. 18). (With No. 66, Michael Billmeyer became the publisher alone.)
　　　Nos. 71 (Oct. 16) – 74 (Nov. 27).
1788, Nos. 77 (Jan. 8) – 89 (June 24).
　　　Nos. 91 (July 22) – 101 (Dec. 9).
1789, Nos. 103 (Jan. 6) – 128 (Dec. 22).
1790, Nos. 129 (Jan. 5) – 142 (July 6). (With No. 143, the weekly issues commence. The first four numbers have the old serial numbers, but the fifth is marked No. 7, the publisher apparently making a mistake. He remedies this by two No. 8's (Aug. 24 and Aug. 31) and two No. 10's (Sept. 14 and Sept. 21).)
　　　Nos. 143 (July 20) – 146 (Aug. 10).
　　　Nos. 7 (Aug. 17) – 24 (Dec. 28).
1791, Nos. 26 (Jan. 11) – 76 (Dec. 27).
1792, Nos. 77 (Jan. 3) – 128 (Dec. 25).
1793, Nos. 129 (Jan. 1) – 131 (Jan. 15).

In L. C. (*Non Vidimus*).
1792, No. 78 (Jan. 10).

Seidensticker says the paper continued into the nineteenth century,—a statement which I have not been able to verify. In PC₃ 76 ff. and NUR 538, Billmeyer has a notice that all back subscriptions to the paper must be paid immediately.

Deutsche Zeitung. Published by Matthias Bärtgis in Friedrich-Stadt, Maryland, in 1786. (No copies discovered and name not known.)

We quote Mr. C. S. Brigham in the *Proceedings of the American Antiquarian Society* of the year 1915:

In the *Maryland Chronicle* of Jan. 18, 1786, he (Matthias Bärtgis) announced his intention of establishing a post " to carry my English and German Newspapers" to nearby towns. Another advertisement in the same paper, dated June 4, 1787, advertises for a partner to take the management of the " Printing-Office in the English and German language, and two public papers in this town."

How long the paper existed is not known.

Baltimore Deutsche Zeitung (weekly). Published 1786 by Henry Dulheuer. (Name unknown and no copies discovered.)

The *Proceedings of the American Antiquarian Society* (1915, p. 156) has this quotation of an advertisement in the *Maryland Journal* of June 16, 1786.

The subscriber respectfully informs his Friends in particular and the Public in general, that he commenced the Publication of his German Newspaper yesterday, and intends to continue it

Weekly. Subscriptions for the same are taken in by him, at his Printing Office in Market Street, nearly opposite the Green-Tree, at the small Price of Ten Shillings per Annum; Five Shillings of which is paid at the time of Subscribing, the better to enable him to prosecute his Undertaking. All Kinds of Printing, in German, performed by Henry Dulheuer, Baltimore, June 15, 1786.

Neue Unpartheyische Lancäster Zeitung und Anzeigsnachrichten. Published by Stiemer, Albrecht und Lahn.

In Lancaster Co. Historical Society (Vidimus July, 1917).

1787, Nos. 1 (Aug. 8) – 21 (Dec. 26) (mutilated No. 17).
1788, Nos. 22 (Jan. 2) – 74 (Dec. 31). (With No. 37, the firm's name became Albrecht und Lahn.)
1789, Nos. 75 (Jan. 7) – 126 (Dec. 30) (mutilated No. 126).
1790, Nos. 127 (Jan. 6) – 178 (Dec. 29). (With No. 137, the firm's name became Johann Albrecht und Comp.)
1791, Nos. 179 (Jan. 5) – 230 (Dec. 28).
1792, Nos. 231 (Jan. 4) – 282 (Dec. 26).
1793, Nos. 283 (Jan. 2) – 314 (Aug. 7). (At the beginning of 1798, the name of the paper was changed to *Der Deutsche Porcupein und Lancäster Anzeigsnachrichten*, with new numbers.)
1799, Nos. 77 (June 19), 104 (Dec. 25). (At the beginning of 1800, the name of the paper was changed to *Der Americanische Staatsbothe und Lancäster Anzeigsnachricten*, the numbering being a continuation of *Der Deutsche Porcupein*.)
1800, Nos. 109 (Jan. 29) – 154 (Dec. 10) (mutilated Nos. 109 and 110). (Two copies of No. 122. No paper published on September 24.)
Nos. 156 (Dec. 24) – 157 (Dec. 31).

In L. C. (Vidimus, Feb. and March, 1917).

1787, Nos. 1 (Aug. 8) – 21 (Dec. 26).
1788, Nos. 22 (Jan. 2) – 74 (Dec. 31).
1789, Nos. 75 (Jan. 7) – 99 (June 24) (mutilated No. 87).
Nos. 101 (July 8) – 126 (Dec. 30).
1790, Nos. 127 (Jan. 6) – 178 (Dec. 29).
1791, Nos. 179 (Jan. 5) – 180 (Jan. 12).

As "Der Deutsche Porcupein."

1798, Nos. 1 (Jan. 3) – 9 (Feb. 28).
    Nos. 11 (Mar. 14) –13 (Mar. 28).
    Nos. 15 (Apr. 11) – 24 (June 13).
    Nos. 26 (June 27) – 36 (Sept. 5).
    Nos. 38 (Sept. 19) – 46 (Nov. 14).
    No. 48 (Nov. 28).
    No. 50 (Dec. 12) – 52 (Dec. 26).
1799, Nos. 53 (Jan. 2) – 104 (Dec. 25).

In Mr. A. K. Hostetter's Private Library, Lancaster, Pa. (Vidimus July, 1917).

1789, Nos. 78 (Jan. 28) – 97 (June 10).
    Nos. 99 (June 24) – 126 (Dec. 30) (mutilated Nos. 100, 105 and 106).
1790, Nos. 127 (Jan. 6) – 154 (July 14) (mutilated No. 154).

In State Library at Harrisburg, Pa. (Vidimus July, 1917).

1790, Nos. 161 (Sept. 1) – 162 (Sept. 8).
    Nos. 164 (Sept 22) – 178 (Dec. 29).
1791, Nos. 180 (Jan. 12) – 221 (Oct. 26) (mutilated No. 221).
1792, Nos. 242 (Mar. 21) – 255 (June 20) (mutilated No. 242).
    Nos. 257 (July 4) (mutilated), 260 (July 25).

In the Harvard College Library (Vidimus Oct., 1917).

1787, Nos. 9 (Oct. 3) – 14 (Nov. 7).
    Nos. 16 (Nov. 21) – 18 (Dec. 5).
    Nos. 20 (Dec. 19) – 21 (Dec. 26).
1788, Nos. 22 (Jan. 2), 24 (Jan. 16), 26 (Jan. 30).
    Nos. 28 (Feb. 13), 31 (Mar. 5) – 34 (Mar. 26).
    Nos. 36 (Apr. 9), 38 (Apr. 23).
1793, No. 335 (Dec. 25).

Neue Unpartheyische Readinger Zeitung und Anzeigsnachrichten. Published by Johnson, Barton und Jungmann.

In the Berks Co. Historical Society, Reading, Pa. (Vidimus, July and August, 1917).

1789, Nos. 1 (Feb. 18) – 8 (Apr. 8).
    Nos. 10 (Apr. 22) – 46 (Dec. 30).

1790, Nos. 47 (Jan. 6) – 48 (Jan. 13).
    Nos. 50 (Jan. 27) – 60 (Apr. 7).
    Nos. 62 (Apr. 21) – 70 (June 16).
    Nos. 72 (June 30) – 74 (July 14).
    Nos. 81 (Sept. 1) – 96 (Dec. 15). (With No. 81, the company's name is Barton und Jungmann. Probably this change occurred with the issue of August 18, because an advertisement in No. 81 announcing the dissolution of the old partnership is dated August 18, 1790.)
    No. 98 (Dec. 29).
1791, Nos. 99 (Jan. 5) – 108 (Mar. 9).
    Nos. 110 (Mar. 23) – 111 (Mar. 30).
    Nos. 113 (Apr. 13) – 133 (Aug. 31).
    Nos. 135 (Sept. 14) – 145 (Nov. 23).
    Nos. 147 (Dec. 7), 149 (Dec. 21), 150 (Dec. 28).
1792, Nos. 151 (Jan. 4) – 159 (Feb. 29).
    Nos. 161 (Mar. 14) – 162 (Mar. 21).
    Nos. 164 (Apr. 4) – 202 (Dec. 26).
1793, Nos. 203 (Jan. 2) – 204 (Jan. 9).
    Nos. 206 (Jan. 23) – 242 (Oct. 2). (With No. 227, the firm's name became Jungmann und Gruber.)
    Nos. 244 (Oct. 16) – 254 (Dec. 25).
1794, Nos. 255 (Jan. 1) – 272 (Apr. 30).
    Nos. 274 (May 14) – 307 (Dec. 31).
1795, Nos. 308 (Jan. 7) – 312 (Feb. 4). (With No. 308, the firm's name became Gottlob Jungmann und Comp.)
    Nos. 314 (Feb. 18) – 330 (June 10).
    Nos. 332 (June 24) – 338 (Aug. 5).
    Nos. 340 (Aug. 19) – 359 (Dec. 30).
1796, Nos. 360 (Jan. 6) – 411 (Dec. 28).
1797, Nos. 412 (Jan. 4) – 463 (Dec. 27).
1798, Nos. 464 (Jan. 3) – 515 (Dec. 26).
1799, Nos. 516 (Jan. 2) – 567 (Dec. 24).
1800, Nos. 568 (Jan. 1) – 597 (July 23). (With No. 573, the firm's name became Jungmann und Brückmann.)
    Nos. 599 (Aug. 6) – 613 (Nov. 12).
    Nos. 616 (Dec. 3) – (Dec. 31).
    Stray number, – No. 276 (May 28, 1794).

In L. C. (Vidimus, Feb., 1917).

1799, Nos. 516 (Jan. 2) – 567 (Dec. 24).
1800, Nos. 568 (Jan. 1) – 620 (Dec. 31).

In the Harvard College Library (Vidimus, Oct., 1917).
1797, Nos. 423 (Mar. 22), 457 (Nov. 15).

In the Possession of Mr. C. W. Unger, Pottsville, Pa., on August 16, 1917 (Non Vidimus).

Copies from 1789 to 1793.

In A. A. S. (Vidimus, Oct., 1917).
1794, Nos. 255 (Jan. 1), 258 (Jan. 22), 259 (Jan. 29).
No. 277 (June 5) (mutilated).

Der General Post-Bothe an die Deutsche Nation in Amerika (semi-weekly). Published by Melchior Steiner for C. C. Reiche, in Philadelphia.

In the Berks Co., Historical Society, Reading, Pa. (Vidimus, Aug., 1917).
1789, Nov. 27 (Prospectus).
1790, Nos. 1 (Jan. 5) – 50 (June 29) (This file is complete).

In L. C. (Vidimus, Feb., 1917).
1789, Nov. 27 (Prospectus).
1790, Nos. 1 (Jan. 5) – 7 (Jan. 26).
    Nos. 9 (Feb. 2) – 40 (May 25).
    Nos. 43 (June 4) – 48 (June 22).

The last number appeared on June 29, 1790.

Die Chesnuthiller Wochenschrift (weekly). Published by Samuel Saur at Chestnut Hill.

In the Locust St. branch of the Philadelphia Library Company (Vidimus, Sept., 1917).
1790, No.   (Oct. 8) Two copies, Prospectus.
    Nos. 1 (Dec. 15) – 3 (Dec. 29).
1791, Nos. 4 (Jan. 5) – 23 (June 7).
    Nos. 26 (June 28) – 28 (July 12).
    Nos. 30 (July 26) – 32 (Aug. 9).
    Nos. 34 (Aug. 23) – 52 (Dec. 27).
1792, Nos. 53 (Jan. 3) – 58 (Feb. 7).
    Nos. 61 (Feb. 28) – 83 (July 31).

Nos. 85 (Aug. 14), 88 (Sept. 4) – 91 (Sept. 25).
Nos. 94 (Oct. 16) – 96 (Oct. 30).
Nos. 98 (Nov. 13) – 102 (Dec. 11), 104 (Dec. 25).
1793, Nos. 105 (Jan. 1) – 108 (Jan. 22).
Nos. 115 (Mar. 12), 116 (Mar. 19), 122 (Apr. 30).
Nos. 123 (May 7), 125 (May 21), 126 (May 28), 128 (June 11).
Nos. 129 (June 18), 133 (July 16), 134 (July 23).
No. 137 (Aug. 13).

In New York Public Library (Non Vidimus).
1793, No. 138 (Aug. 20).

Seidensticker (First Century of German Printing in America, pp. 137 and 138) says Saur moved to Philadelphia sometime in 1794 and continued the paper for a short time at that place under the name of *Das Philadelphier Wochenblat.*

Neuer Unpartheyischer Eastoner Bothe und Northamptoner Kundschafter (weekly). Published at Easton, Pa., by Jacob Weygandt and Son.

The only issue before 1801 that I discovered is a photographic fac-simile in the possession of Mr. Ethan Allen Weaver of Germantown, Pa. The copy bears the date of Nov. 13, 1798, Number 270.

General Staats-Bothe, mit den Neuesten Fremden, Einheimischen, und Gemeinnützigen Nachrichten, an die Deutsche Nation in America (bi-weekly). Published by Matthias Bärtgis in Frederick, Maryland, 1793. (No copies discovered.)

The following is taken from an advertisement in PC$_2$ 201.

In Friederichstaun, Maryland, giebt Herr Matthäus Bärtges, Buchdrucker, der sich mit lobenswerthem Eifer, und Anopferung bemüht, die Deutsche Sprache aufrecht zu erhalten, seith dem Anfang dieses Jahrs, alle 14 Tage einen grossen Bogen heraus, unter dem Titel, "General Staats-Bothe, mit den Neuesten Fremden, Einheimischen, und Gemeinnützigen Nachrichten, an die Deutsche Nation in America."

In C. W. 129, we find an article taken "aus dem General Staats-Bothen von Friedrichs-Stadt, Maryland."

Seidensticker (p. 135 in "The First Century of German Printing in America") surmises that this may be the same paper as the one published by Bärtgis in 1786 and 1787 in Fredericktown, but the advertisement in PC$_2$ 201, quoted above, seems to indicate that this paper started with the beginning of 1793.

Der Neue Unpartheyische Baltimore Bote und Maryland Staats-Register (weekly). Published by Samuel Saur, Baltimore, Maryland.

In the Baltimore City Library (Non Vidimus).
1796, No. 59 (May 4).

According to this, the first number probably appeared on Wednesday, March 25, 1795.

In 1799 Saur was publishing a newspaper three times per week, as may be seen from the following advertisement found in his almanac for the year 1800.

Der Herausgeber dieses Calenders bedienet sich gleichfalls dieser Gelegenheit, dem geehrten Publikum kund zu thun, dasz er wieder seith geraumer Zeit eine deutsche Zeitung herausgiebt und zwar dreymal die Woche auf einen (sic) grossen halben Bogen, für zwey und einen halben Thaler des Jahrs, oder zwölf Schilling und sechs Pens für zwey Zeitungen wöchentlich; da aber das Postgeld für einen halben Bogen eben so viel beträgt als für einen ganzen Bogen, und desfalls seinen ehemaligen Kunden in der Entfernung zu hoch im Preisz zu stehen kommt, so hat er sich entschlossen, (im Fall sich eine ansehnliche Zahl Subscribenten zeitlich einfinden sollten) bis den ersten Februar 1800 eine Wöchentliche Zeitung Bogen gross herauszugeben, für ein und einen halben Thaler den Jahrgang.

Die Westliche Correspondenz, und Hägerstauner Wochenschrift (weekly). Published by Johann Gruber at Hagerstown, Maryland.

<small>In Berks Co. Historical Society, Reading, Pa. (*Vidimus, Aug., 1917*). 1796, No. 68 (Sept. 28, 1796).</small>

Gruber started a new series in 1799, as may be seen from the issue of March 12, 1801, which is marked No. 90.

References to the paper are found in A 18, 117, 118; PC$_3$ 3, 15; UH 13, 23; DP 65, et al.

Die Unpartheyische York Gazette (weekly). Published by Solomon Mäyer in York, Pa.

<small>In the Harvard College Library (*Vidimus October, 1917*). 1797, Nos. 50 (Jan. 31), 52 (Feb. 14).</small>

On p. 97 of Carter and Glossbrenner's "History of York County," we find the following, "In the spring of that year (1796) Solomon Meyer commenced the publication of a German paper entitled, *Die York Gazette*. This was the first paper printed in this county in the German language." The same statement is made in Prowell's "History of York County" (Vol. I, p. 549).

References to the paper are found in AS 109, 112, 119, 120, 123; PC$_3$ 3, 61, 65; NUR 452, 548; DP 19, et al.

Mr. George R. Prowell of the York County Historical

Society claims that the Society has a complete file from 1796 to 1801, but diligent search by him and by myself failed to reveal it.

Der Unpartheyische Reading Adler (weekly). Published by Jacob Schneider und Georg Gerrisch in Reading, Pa.

Although both Seidensticker (op. cit., p. 145) and Miller ("Early German American Newspapers," p. 53) say the newspaper was started on Nov. 29, 1796, and the history of the *Adler*, as printed in the centennial number (Nov. 28, 1896), states definitely that the first number was printed on Nov. 29, 1796, and the second on January 10, 1797, the truth is that the one published on November 29 was a sample number only and No. 1 was issued on January 3. In No. 22 (December 16, 1796) of the *Impartial Reading Herald* (an English paper published by Schneider), we find an advertisement which states that the first number of the German paper will appear on Tuesday, the third of January next.

In Berks County Historical Society—First Set (*Vidimus, July and August, 1917*).

1797, Nos. 1 (Jan. 3) – 52 (Dec. 26). (With No. 3, the firm name became Jacob Schneider und Comp. and the word "Reading" was changed to "Readinger.")
1798, Nos. 53 (Jan. 2) – 104 (Dec. 25).
1799, Nos. 105 (Jan. 1) – 157 (Dec. 31).
1800, Nos. 158 (Jan. 7) – 209 (Dec. 30).

At the Same Place—Second Set (*Vidimus, July and August, 1917*).

1797, Nos. 1 (Jan. 3) – 52 (Dec. 26).
1798, Nos. 53 (Jan. 2) – 104 (Dec. 25).
1799, Nos. 105 (Jan. 1) – 147 (Oct. 22).
   Stray number, 1798, No. 102 (Dec. 11).

In the A. A. S., Worcester, Mass. (*Vidimus, October, 1917*).

1796, No. 1 (Nov. 29) (prospectus).

1797, Nos. 2 (Jan. 10) – 52 (Dec. 26).
1798, Nos. 53 (Jan. 2) – 104 (Dec. 25).
1799, Nos. 148 (Oct. 29) – 157 (Dec. 31).
1800, Nos. 158 (Jan. 7) – 209 (Dec. 30).

Die Pennsylvanische Wochenschrift (weekly). Published by Stellingius (?) und Lepper in Hanover, Pa. (No copies discovered.)

From Carter and Glossbrenner's History of York County, p. 100:

The first paper printed in Hanover was a German one entitled *Die Pennsylvanische Wochenschrift*, the first number of which was issued by Lepper and Stellinius (sic), in April 1797. Mr. Lepper became not long afterwards, the sole proprietor of the establishment and he continued the paper until February, 1805.

The same statement occurs on page 557, Vol. I of Prowell's "History of York County," except that he says the publishers were W. D. Lepper and E. Stettinius, both educated Germans who had learned the art of printing in the Fatherland.

Seidensticker (op. cit., p. 147) names "Stellingius und Lepper" as the publishers.

In PC_3 of July 30, 1800, W. D. Lepper is mentioned as one of the pall bearers at the funeral of the semi-weekly *Pennsylvanische Correspondenz*.

Die Pennsylvanische Correspondenz (semi-weekly). Published by Heinrich Schweitzer in Philadelphia.

In the Library of W. J. Hinke, Auburn, N. Y.

1798, No. 57 (April 24) (vidimus, Oct. 24, 1917).
(Hence the first number probably appeared on October 10, 1797.)

Full column advertisements dated August 1, 1797, in A 33 and NUR 443, about the proposed paper which is to be issued twice a week by Heinrich Schweitzer.

The paper is mentioned in H 40; DP 56; PC_3 14, 15, 44, 66, 67, 68, 69, 70, 73, 78, July 30, 1800, et al.

In the PC_4 issue of July 30, 1800, there is an article with black borders entitled "Ach wie betrübt." It announces that the *Pennsylvanische Correspondenz* will appear as a semi-weekly for the last time on Friday (presumably August 1) and that thereafter it will be continued weekly.

Philadelphisches Magazin oder Unterhaltender Gesellschafter für die Deutschen in Amerika (quarterly). Published by Henrich und Joseph R. Kämmerer jun. in Philadelphia.

In P. H. S. (Vidimus, Sept., 1917).
1798, No. 1 (May 1).

A second number was issued in August, 1798, according to an advertisement in PC_3 17. These two numbers were probably the only ones published. Shortly after the appearance of the second number, the terrible yellow fever epidemic of 1798 broke out in Philadelphia, among the victims of which were Henrich Kämmerer and a younger brother.

Des Landmanns Wochenblatt, neuer und gemeinnüzlicher Nachrichten (weekly). Published by Wm. Hamilton and Conrad Wortmann, Lancaster, Pa. (1798–1799). Suspended publication on February 19, 1799. (No copies found.)

In the *Lancaster Journal* (Vol. IV, No. 33), January 27, 1798, is an advertisement of this paper, which is to be started by Wm. Hamilton and Conrad Wortmann at the beginning of February. Hamilton says he has made a contract with a man who came from Germany. Price of paper $1.50.

In DP 62 we find a notice that on February 19 (1799), the *Landmanns Wochenblatt* when only one year old died. On the 26th appeared another Jacobin child "nach einem verjüngten Maasstab und in einem allerliebst niedlichen Taschenformat, ob dieses Kind seines Vaters ein höheres Alter erreichen wird, stehet zu erwarten."

The last mentioned newspaper is the *Lancäster Wochenblatt* (q. v.).

The *Landmanns Wochenblatt* is also mentioned in DP 35, 53, 56, 83; NUR 492; A 79; PC$_3$ 4, 17, et al.

Das Lancaster Wochenblatt (weekly). Published by Wm. Hamilton in Lancaster, Pa., from February 26, 1799, to May of the same year. (No copies found.) Successor to *Landmanns Wochenblatt* (q. v.).

In DP 83, in a communication signed by "Von einem sogenannten Tory"—

Als ich am letztern Samstag nach Lancaster kam, ist mir eine neue Miszgeburt zu Gesicht gekommen, nemlich eine Deutsche Franzosenzeitung, ehemals Landmanns Wochenblatt und nachgehends *Lancaster Wochenblatt* genannt, welche beyde Ungeheuer vom Jacobiner Gift ergriffen, die Schwindsucht bekommen, und weilen sie französische Werkzeuge waren, abgestorben sind; und nun erscheint diese Zeitung unter dem Namen des Lancaster Correspondenten.

In H 1, we are told that the *Lancaster Correspondent*

has taken over the subscribers of the *Lancaster Wochenblatt*.

Die Subscribenten zum *Lancaster Wochenblatt* die beym Anfang desselben auf ein halb Jahr bey Herrn Hamilton voraus bezahlt haben, und nun Subscribenten zu dem Lancaster Correspondenten geworden sind, werden ersucht jeder einen viertel Thaler an mich noch zu bezahlen, welcher denn die 6 monatliche Vorausbezahlung ausmacht.

Das Neue monatliche Readinger Magazin, für den Bürger und Land-Mann (monthly). Published by Jacob Schneider und Comp. (No copies found.)

First number dated February, 1799, although it was not issued much before March.

Advertisement of proposals for new magazine in A 95 ff.

Advertisement that the new magazine is about ready for press in A 105 ff.

Advertisement that the first number has left the press in A 114 ff.

I have been unable to find any mention of a second number.

Unpartheyische Härrisburg Morgenröthe Zeitung (weekly). Published by B. Mayer und C. Fahnestock.

Seidensticker in his " First Century of German Printing in America," p. 137, quoting Dr. Wm. H. Egle's "History of Dauphin and Lebanon Counties," says that the first number was published on March 1, 1794. Whether this statement is true is doubtful, because, in No. 1 of March 12, 1799, the publishers do not allude to any previous paper, and in No. 52 (March 3, 1800), we read,

"Diese Woche beschliesset die 52te Nummer, nachdem wir angefangen Zeitungen zu drucken, das erste Jahr." It may be that Mayer and Fahnestock issued a sample number on March 1, 1794, and did not continue because of lack of encouragement.

In the State Library at Harrisburg (Vidimus, July, 1917).

First Set.
1799, Nos. 1 (Mar. 12) – 5 (Apr. 9).
    Nos. 7 (Apr. 23) – 20 (July 23).
    Nos. 22 (Aug. 6) – 43 (Dec. 30). (Beginning with No. 22 the publisher was Benjamin Mayer.)
1800, Nos. 44 (Jan. 6) – 64 (May 26).
    Nos. 66 (June 9) – 95 (Dec. 29). (No. 75 the title was *Die Härrisburg Morgenröthe Zeitung*. On and after No. 76, the name was *Die Härrisburg Zeitung*.)

At the Same Place (Vidimus, July, 1917).

Second Set.
1799, Nos. 1 (Mar. 12) – 4 (Apr. 2).
    Nos. 6 (Apr. 16) – 43 (Dec. 30).
1800, Nos. 44 (Jan. 6) – 95 (Dec. 29).

Der Lancaster Correspondent (weekly). Published by C. J. Hütter.

In Lancaster County Historical Society (Vidimus, July, 1917).
1799, Nos. 1 (May 25) – 32 (Dec. 28).
1800, Nos. 33 (Jan. 4) – 84 (Dec. 27).

In P. H. S. (Vidimus, September, 1917).
1799, Nos. 1 (May 25) – 32 (Dec. 28) (No. 1 mutilated).
1800, Nos. 33 (Jan. 4) – 84 Dec. 27).

In Berks County Historical Society, Reading, Pa. (Vidimus, August, 1917).
1800, Nos. 40 (Feb. 22) – 43 (Mar. 15).
    Nos. 45 (Mar. 29) – 54 (May 31).
    Nos. 56 (June 14) – 60 (July 12).
    Nos. 62 (July 26) – 63 (Aug. 2).

Nos. 66 (Aug. 23) – 67 (Aug. 30).
Nos. 69 (Sept. 13) – 72 (Oct. 4).
Nos. 74 (Oct. 13) – 75 (Oct. 25).
Nos. 78 (Nov. 15) – 84 (Dec. 27).

Der Volksberichter (weekly). Published by A. Billmeyer in York, Pa. (No copies found.)

In Carter and Glossbrenner's "History of York County" (p. 97), we read:

The paper next established in the borough of York, was, *Der Volksberichter*, the first number of which was published by Andrew Billmeyer on the 25th of July, 1799.

Prowell in his "History of York County" says the same.

In PC$_3$ 65, mention is made of the *Volksberichter's* issue of September 26, 1799, No. 10. Assuming that the paper had been published regularly every week, this would indicate that the first number appeared on July 25, 1799, thus corroborating Carter and Glossbrenner.

In UH 24, a writer, signing himself "Kein Deist," says that it is reported the *Volksberichter* is edited by Rev. Görring of York.

The paper is mentioned in AS 112, 119; UH 76; NUR 550, 602, 584; A 173. (Art. from the *York Gazette* mentions Yorktauner *Volksvernichter* and talks about "die Zeitungsprediger und Volksbetrüger."

Die Philadelphische Correspondenz (thrice a week city edition). Published by Joseph R. Kämmerer und G. Helmbold, jun. (February 11, 1800–April 5, 1800 ?). (No copies found.)

The publishers intend to publish a thrice-a-week city

edition at a maximum cost of $3.00 per year as soon as they have 500 subscribers. They will continue to publish the country (weekly) edition.—PC$_3$ 67 ff.

On Tuesday, February 11, 1800, the publishers intend to issue the first number of the thrice-a-week edition.—PC$_3$ 79.

Notice of dissolution of partnership, dated March 4, 1800. Helmbold assures his readers that he will continue to publish the paper thrice-a-week, "wie seith einiger Zeit."—PC$_3$ 83.

In an article dated March 27, 1800, Helmbold warns his readers that he will have to discontinue the city edition within a short time, unless they will secure more subscribers for him.—PC$_3$ 87.

For reasons why the last number probably appeared on April 5, see under "Gemeinnützige Philadelphische Correspondenz."

Were They Ever Published?

Under this heading I want to mention some German papers which may have been published, although I lack conclusive evidence that they ever appeared. References to them have come down to us in three ways: first, through advertisements in which publishers announced that they intended to start the publication of a paper; second, through vague references in contemporary newspapers; third, through the works of writers living after the time when the papers were supposed to have been published.

The earliest one of these papers is said to have been published between 1759 and 1762 in Philadelphia by Weiss and Miller. Thomas (op. cit., Vol. II, p. 147) says that it was a continuation of Franklin and Armbruster's *Phila-*

delphische Zeitung and that Armbruster was again the publisher of it in 1762–1764. We know, however, that the title of Armbruster's paper was *Die Pennsylvanische Fama*. It is difficult to decide whether Weiss and Miller ever published a paper, since our only evidence is the statement by Thomas, who is at times very unreliable in his discussion of the German papers. The firm of Miller and Weiss was publishing during the period in question the almanac which Armbruster had issued while he was publisher of the *Philadelphische Zeitung*.

In Miller's *Staatsbote* of August 6, 1764, I find an article on lightning rods. The writer claims that they are very useful, "wie man noch kürzlich in der Englischen und Deutschen Zeitung von Boston gelesen." So far as I know, there is no other reference to a bi-lingual paper in Boston. Mr. Clarence S. Brigham of the American Antiquarian Society does not believe that it ever existed. The question is, does the word "Zeitung" here mean newspaper or news? The probabilities certainly favor the former interpretation.

In March, 1776, the firm of Steiner and Cist of Philadelphia announced (see S 645 and M 781) that they would start a paper as soon as they would have obtained five hundred subscribers. The paper was probably never started, although I have found no statement to that effect.

Fourteen years later, Charles Cist proposed to begin a semi-weekly German paper in Philadelphia, *Neue Philadelphische Zeitung*. (See PC 486, NUL 157–160, and Cist's German almanac for 1791.) This paper also probably never materialized.

More interest is attached to an advertisement in the Harrisburg *Oracle of Dauphin* of July 22, 1793, in which the firm Allen and Wyeth announce the intention of starting a German paper on October 1, 1793, if they could secure four hundred and fifty subscribers. As we have seen, some writers claim that Mayer and Fahnestock started the publication of the *Morgenröthe Zeitung* on March 1, 1794. Although the publishers' statement seems to contradict this, we might harmonize the two statements by supposing that Allen and Wyeth began their paper on March 1, 1794, and that Mayer and Fahnestock succeeded them in 1799. I have, however, absolutely no proof of this.

On November 29, 1796, Solomon Mäyer, publisher of the *York Gazette*, and a man by the name of Plitt issued a circular containing proposals for a German daily paper in Philadelphia and for a weekly paper in York and Philadelphia. The title of the former was to be *Pennsylvanische Zeitung und täglicher Anzeiger*, and of the latter *Pennsylvanische Zeitung und wöchentlicher Anzeiger*. Presumably the proposals were never carried into effect, although I cannot be positive of this since I had no opportunity to examine many Philadelphia German papers of 1797 for possible references to the paper. However, these proposals are interesting because they show the first attempt to establish a German daily in America.

In a foot-note to page 93 of Miller's "Early German American Newspapers," the statement is made that a German paper, *The Farmers' Register* was established in Chambersburg, Pennsylvania, by Snowden and McCorcle on April 19, 1798. However, this is almost certainly erroneous. An English paper with this name was started by the firm in 1798 or 1799; but I did not find any mention of a German paper, although I examined the issues of the

English paper, found in the library of the Historical Society of Pennsylvania. After the removal of the firm to Greensburg, proposals were made to start a German paper, but according to the advertisement the first number appeared at the beginning of January, 1801.

TABLE I.

The following pages show the number of copies of newspapers found which were published prior to 1801, and the libraries where they are now preserved.

Year	Philadelphische Zeitung in Pa. Hist. Soc.	Philadelphische Zeitung (facsimile).	S in Pennsylvania Historical Society.	S in Library of S. W. Pennypacker.	S in American Philosophical Society	S in Library of Dr. George Hetrich.	Die Lancastersche Zeitung in Pa. Hist. Soc.	PZ in Pennsylvania Historical Society.	Total by Years.
1732	1	1	..	..	..	..	..	..	2
1739	..	..	1	..	..	..	..	..	1
1742	..	..	1	..	..	..	..	..	1
1743	..	..	9	1	..	..	..	..	10
1744	..	..	12	12*	..	..	..	..	24
1745	..	..	12	11*	..	..	..	..	23
1746	..	..	12	..	..	..	..	..	12
1747	..	..	12	..	6	..	..	..	18
1748	..	..	16	..	16	..	..	..	32
1749	..	..	19	..	19	..	..	..	38
1750	..	..	20	..	20	..	..	..	40
1751	..	..	23	..	23	..	..	..	46
1752	..	..	23	..	22	..	5	..	50
1753	..	..	3	..	22	..	1	..	26
1754	..	..	13	..	..	..	..	..	13
1755	..	..	23	20*	..	..	..	2	45
1756	..	..	25	26*	..	..	..	3	54
1757	..	..	26	26*	..	..	..	24	76
1758	..	..	26	..	..	..	..	..	26
1759	..	..	24	..	..	..	..	..	24
1760	..	..	7	..	..	..	..	..	7
1761	..	..	20	..	..	..	..	..	20
1762	..	..	2	..	..	..	..	..	2
1763	..	..	..	..	..	..	..	..	..
1764	..	..	..	..	..	..	..	..	..
1765	..	..	..	..	..	..	..	..	..
1766	..	..	1	..	..	..	..	..	1
1767	..	..	..	..	..	..	..	..	..
1768	..	..	..	..	..	..	..	..	..
1769	..	..	..	..	..	..	..	..	..
1770	..	..	..	..	..	..	..	..	..
1771	..	..	..	..	..	..	..	..	..
1772	..	..	..	..	..	..	..	..	..
1773	..	..	..	..	..	..	..	..	..
1774	..	..	..	..	..	..	..	..	..
1775	..	..	1	..	..	..	..	..	1
1776	..	..	2	..	..	..	..	..	2
1777	..	..	1	..	..	1	..	..	2
1778	..	..	..	..	..	..	..	..	..
1779	..	..	..	..	..	..	..	..	..
1780	..	..	..	..	..	..	..	..	..
Total	1	1	334	96*	128	1	6	29	596
	2		559				6	29	

* Approximate number.

Year	Amount Brought Forward by Years.	M in Archives of Deutsche Gesell.	M in Ridgway Branch of Philadelphia Library Company.	M in Library of Congress.	M in Pennsylvania Historical Society.	M in Possession of Dr. W. J. Campbell.	Der Pennsylvanische Staats-Courier (reprint).	Ba in Pennsylvania Historical Society.	Ba in Library of Congress.	Pennsylvanische Gazette in Library of Congress.	Pennsylvanische Gazette in Pa. Hist. Society.	PS in American Philo. Society.	PS in New York Public Library.	Total by Years.
1732	2													2
1739	1													1
1742	1													1
1743	10													10
1744	24													24
1745	23													23
1746	12													12
1747	18													18
1748	32													32
1749	38													38
1750	40													40
1751	46													46
1752	50													50
1753	26													26
1754	13													13
1755	45													45
1756	54													54
1757	76													76
1758	26													26
1759	24													24
1760	7													7
1761	20													20
1762	2	50			1									53
1763			34											34
1764			52											52
1765			49											49
1766	1		52											53
1767			52	2	2									56
1768			52		1									53
1769			52		1									53
1770			51		20									71
1771			53		45									98
1772			52	13	44									109
1773			51	45	52									148
1774			52	41	51									144
1775	1		83		85									169
1776	2		80	1	79									162
1777	2		35	1	35									73
1778			21		21	1	1	21	2					67
1779			21		15					2	1	3		42
1780												1	1	2
Total	596	50	842	104	451	1	1	21	2	2	1	4	1	2,076
			1448			1		23		3		5		

Year	PC, PC₂, PC₃, PC₄ in the Pennsylvania Historical Society.	PC in American Philosophical Soc.	PC₂ in the State Library at Harrisburg.	PC, PC₂ in Krauth Mem. Lib.	PC, PC₂ in Library of Congress.	PC, PC₂ in the Harvard College Library.	PC, PC₂, PC₃ in Library of Dr. W. J. Hinke.	PC₂ in American Antiquarian Soc.	GZ, GZ₂ in the Pa. Hist. Soc.	GZ₂ in the Library of Congress.	NUL, DP, AS in Lanc. Co. Hist. Society.	NUL, DP in the Library of Congress.	NUL in Library of Mr. A. K. Hostetter.	NUL in State Library at Harrisburg.	NUL in Harvard College Library.	Total by Years.
1781	24	...	...	2	1	...	...	...	...	...	...	...	...	...	...	27
1782	53	...	...	1	...	...	...	...	...	...	...	...	...	...	...	54
1783	34	10	...	2	1	...	...	...	...	...	...	...	...	...	...	47
1784	33	34	...	...	...	...	...	...	...	...	...	...	...	...	...	67
1785	...	23	...	...	...	35	...	...	14	...	...	...	...	...	...	72
1786	29	22	...	2	...	2	...	...	15	...	...	...	...	...	...	70
1787	43	2	...	...	3	...	...	...	23	...	21	21	...	...	11	124
1788	43	...	...	...	...	...	...	...	24	...	53	53	...	...	10	183
1789	12	...	...	2	...	...	...	...	26	...	52	51	48	...	...	191
1790	28	...	...	...	2	...	2	...	38	...	52	52	28	17	...	219
1791	100	...	101	...	...	1	2	...	51	...	52	2	...	42	...	351
1792	50	...	59	1	...	...	1	...	52	1	52	...	...	16	...	232
1793	49	...	73	...	...	...	...	...	3	...	32	...	...	...	1	158
1794	20	...	103	2	2	...	4	2	...	...	...	...	...	...	...	133
1795	11	...	102	...	1	16	...	...	...	...	...	...	...	...	...	130
1796	10	...	98	...	1	4	...	3	...	...	...	...	...	...	...	116
1797	...	...	...	...	...	1	...	...	...	...	...	...	...	...	...	1
1798	27	...	...	...	...	...	...	...	...	...	...	46	...	...	...	73
1799	43	...	...	...	...	...	...	...	...	...	2	52	...	...	...	97
1800	12	...	...	...	...	...	1	...	...	...	49	...	...	...	...	62
Total	621	91	536	12	11	59	10	5	246	1	365	277	76	75	22	2,407

1,345   247   815

Were They Ever Published?

Year	Amount Brought Forward by Years.	NUR in Berks County Historical Society.	NUR in Library of Congress.	NUR in Harvard College Library.	NUR in American Antiquarian Society.	NUR in Library of Chas. W. Unger.	GP in Berks County Historical Society.	GP in Library of Congress.	CW in Locust Street Branch of Phila. Library Company.	CW in New York Public Library.	Eastoner Bothe (facsimile).	UII in State Library at Harrisburg.	Total by Years.
1781	27	...	...	...	...	...	...	...	...	...	...	...	27
1782	54	...	...	...	...	...	...	...	...	...	...	...	54
1783	47	...	...	...	...	...	...	...	...	...	...	...	47
1784	67	...	...	...	...	...	...	...	...	...	...	...	67
1785	72	...	...	...	...	...	...	...	...	...	...	...	72
1786	70	...	...	...	...	...	...	...	...	...	...	...	70
1787	124	...	...	...	...	...	...	...	...	...	...	...	124
1788	183	...	...	...	...	...	...	...	...	...	...	...	183
1789	191	45	...	...	...	45*	1	1	...	...	...	...	283
1790	219	42	...	...	...	50*	50	45	5	...	...	...	411
1791	351	47	...	...	...	50*	...	...	45	...	...	...	493
1792	232	50	...	...	...	50*	...	...	43	...	...	...	373
1793	158	50	...	...	...	50*	...	...	15	1	...	...	274
1794	133	53	...	...	4	...	...	...	...	...	...	...	190
1795	130	49	...	...	...	...	...	...	...	...	...	...	179
1796	116	52	...	...	...	...	...	...	...	...	...	...	168
1797	1	52	...	2	...	...	...	...	...	...	...	...	55
1798	73	52	...	...	...	...	...	...	...	...	1	...	126
1799	97	52	52	...	...	...	...	...	...	...	...	83	284
1800	62	50	53	...	...	...	...	...	...	...	...	103	268
Total	2,407	594	105	2	4	245*	51	46	108	1	1	186	3,750
		950					97		109		1	186	

*Approximate number.

210   The Pennsylvania-German Society.

Year.	Amount Brought Forward by Years.	Baltimore Bote in Baltimore City Library.	Westliche Correspondenz in Berks Co. Hist. Soc.	York Gazette in Harvard College Library.	A in Berks County Historical Society.	A in American Antiquarian Society.	Pennsylvanische Correspondenz in Libr. of W. J. Hinke.	Philadelphisches Magazin in Pa. Hist. Soc.	H in Lancaster County Historical Society.	H in Pennsylvania Historical Society.	H in Berks County Historical Society.	Total by Years.
Total number of papers up to 1780												2,076
1781...	27	...	...	...	...	...	...	...	...	...	...	27
1782...	54	...	...	...	...	...	...	...	...	...	...	54
1783...	47	...	...	...	...	...	...	...	...	...	...	47
1784...	67	...	...	...	...	...	...	...	...	...	...	67
1785...	72	...	...	...	...	...	...	...	...	...	...	72
1786...	70	...	...	...	...	...	...	...	...	...	...	70
1787...	124	...	...	...	...	...	...	...	...	...	...	124
1788...	183	...	...	...	...	...	...	...	...	...	...	183
1789...	283	...	...	...	...	...	...	...	...	...	...	283
1790...	411	...	...	...	...	...	...	...	...	...	...	411
1791...	493	...	...	...	...	...	...	...	...	...	...	493
1792...	375	...	...	...	...	...	...	...	...	...	...	375
1793...	274	...	...	...	...	...	...	...	...	...	...	274
1794...	190	...	...	...	...	...	...	...	...	...	...	190
1795...	179	...	...	...	...	...	...	...	...	...	...	179
1796...	168	1	1	...	...	1	...	...	...	...	...	171
1797...	55	...	...	2	104	51	...	...	...	...	...	212
1798...	126	...	...	...	105	52	1	1	...	...	...	285
1799...	284	...	...	...	96	10	...	...	32	32	...	454
1800...	268	...	...	...	52	52	...	...	52	52	36	512
Total.	3,750	1	1	2	357	166	1	1	84	84	36	4,483 6,559
		1	1	2	523		1	1	204			

The following copies of Saur's *Geistliches Magazien* have been discovered. This magazine was published at irregular intervals between 1764 and 1774, none of the issues having the date of publication.

In Penna. Hist. Society.......................	50
In the Phila. Library Co.	37
In possession of Wm. J. Campbell..............	48*
In State Library at Harrisburg................	64
In library of M. G. Brumbaugh................	50*
Total...............	249
Total of the other papers......................	6559
Grand total of copies, 1732–1800...............	6808

TABLE II.

The following pages show the number of issues located and examined and the approximate number that were published.

Names of Newspapers.	No. of Issues Examined.	No. of Issues Located.	No. of Issues Published.
Philadelphische Zeitung (1732)	2	2	2*
Saur's Germantown Paper (1739-77)	353	354*	970*
Die Lancastersche Zeitung (1752-53)	6	6	31
Philadelphische Zeitung (1755-57)	29	29	68
Miller's Staatsbote (1762-79)	898	898	920
Ein Geistliches Magazien (1764-74)	54	64	64
Der Pennsylvanische Staats Courier (1777-78)	1	1	30*
Das Pennsylvanische Zeitung (1778)	21	21	21
Die Pennsylvanische Gazette (1779)	1	1	1*
Philadelphisches Staatsregister (1779-81)	4	5	65*
Philadelphische Correspondenz (1781-1800)	993	993	1,310*
Germantauner Zeitung (1785-1800)	246	246	686*
Lancäster Zeitung, etc. (1787-1800)	355	355	700*
Readinger Zeitung (1789-1800)	596	600*	620*
Der General Post Bothe (1790)	51	51	51
Die Chesnuthiller Wochenschrift (1790-1794)	108	109	180*
Eastoner Bothe (1793-1800)	1	1	380*
Baltimore Bote (1795-1800)	0	1	300*
Westliche Correspondenz (1795-1800)	1	1	280*
York Gazette (1796-1800)	2	2	255*
Reading Adler (1796-1800)	210	210	210
Pennsylvanische Correspondenz (1797-1800)	1	1	285*
Philadelphisches Magazin (1798)	1	1	2
Harrisburg Zeitung (1799-1800)	95	95	95
Lancaster Correspondent (1799-1800)	84	84	84
Total number	4,113	4,131	7,620

*Approximate number.

BIBLIOGRAPHY.

In this bibliography there are mentioned only very few of the works on the various phases of the social conditions of the eighteenth century Pennsylvania Germans. For more nearly complete bibliographies the reader is referred to Kuhn's "German and Swiss Settlements in Pennsylvania" and Faust's "The German Element in the United States." Under the heading, "General Works," are found publications containing material on the general subject, while under the chapters are listed those of special bearing on the subjects discussed in the various chapters.

General Works.

Americana Germanica. A quarterly devoted to the comparative study of the literary, linguistic and other cultural relations of Germany and America. 1897–1902. 4 vols. (Continued as *German American Annals,* q. v.)

Beidelman, William. The Story of the Pennsylvania Germans; embracing an account of their origin, their history and their dialect. Easton, Pa., 1898. (Contains many inaccuracies.)

Berks County Historical Society, Proceedings of the.

Carter, W. C. and Glossbrenner, A. J. History of York County from its Erection to the present time. York, Pa., 1834. (Very accurate.)

Claire, I. S. A Brief History of Lancaster County. Lancaster, 1892.

Deutsche Pionier, Der. A monthly magazine published by Der deutsche

Pionier-Verein von Cincinnati. 18 vols. 1869–1887. From 1885 to 1887 it was issued as a quarterly.

Deutsch-Amerikanische Geschichtsblätter. Published by the German American Historical Society of Illinois. 1901–1917. 17 vols.

Deutsch-Amerikanisches Magazin. Edited by H. A. Rattermann. Volume I, 1886.

Egle, William H. History of the Counties of Dauphin and Lebanon in the Commonwealth of Pennsylvania. Philadelphia, 1883.

Eickhoff, Anton. In der neuen Heimath. New York. 1884.

Ellis (Franklin) and Evans (Samuel). History of Lancaster County, Pennsylvania. Philadelphia, 1883.

Faust, A. B. The German Element in the United States. 2 vols. Houghton, Mifflin and Company, 1909.

German American Annals. Continuation of *Americana Germanica.* Published by the German American Historical Society, Philadelphia. 1903–1918. 16 vols.

Hazard, Samuel. The Register of Pennsylvania. Philadelphia. 1828–1832.

Henry, M. S. History of Northampton County. Unpublished Ms. in possession of the Historical Society of Pennsylvania, Philadelphia.

Kelker, Luther R. History of Dauphin County. 3 vols. New York and Chicago, 1907.

Kuhns, Oscar. The German and Swiss Settlements of Colonial Pennsylvania. A Study of the So-called Pennsylvania Dutch. Henry Holt and Company, 1901.

Lancaster County Historical Society, Proceedings of the. (From 1896 to the present time.)

Löher, Franz. Geschichte und Zustände der Deutschen in Amerika. Zweite Ausgabe, Göttingen, 1855.

McMaster, J. B. A History of the People of the United States, From the Revolution to the Civil War. 8 vols. The first two volumes contain reliable information about the eighteenth century Pennsylvania Germans.

Mombert, J. I. An Authentic History of Lancaster County in the State of Pennsylvania. Lancaster, 1869.

Montgomery, M. L. Historical and Biographical Annals of Berks County, Pennsylvania. 2 vols. Chicago, 1909. (Many inaccuracies.)

—— History of Berks County, Pennsylvania. Philadelphia, 1886.

—— School History of Berks County in Pennsylvania. Philadelphia, 1889.

Pennsylvania Archives. Philadelphia and Harrisburg. 1852–1902. (Four series.)

Pennsylvania German, The. A Popular Magazine of Biography, History, Genealogy, Folklore, Literature, etc. 1901–1911. 12 vols.

Pennsylvania German Society, Proceedings of. 1891 to the present time. (27 vols.)
Pennsylvania Magazine of History and Biography, The. Published by the Historical Society of Pennsylvania. 1877–1918. 42 vols.
Prowell, G. R. History of York County, Pennsylvania. 2 vols. Chicago, 1907.
Rush, Benjamin. An account of the manners of the German inhabitants of Pennsylvania, written in 1789. Notes added by I. Daniel Rupp. Philadelphia, 1875.
Scharf, J. T. History of Western Maryland. 2 vols.
Schem, A. J. Deutsch-Amerikanisches Konversations-Lexicon. 11 vols. New York, 1869–1874.
Seidensticker, Oswald. Bilder aus der Deutsch-pennsylvanischen Geschichte. E. Steiger and Co., 1886.
Tenner, A. Der Heutige Standpunkt der Kultur in den Vereinigten Staaten. New York, 1886.

Chapter I.

American Antiquarian Society, Proceedings of. Worcester, Mass., 1812–1917.
American Newspaper Directory, 1776. New York; George P. Rowell and Co., 1876.
Bausman, Lottie M. A Bibliography of Lancaster County, Pennsylvania. 1745–1912. Publication of the Pennsylvania Federation of Historical Societies.
Cassel, A. H. A History of Sower's Newspaper. (MS. in the possession of the Historical Society of Pennsylvania.)
Dapp, C. F. Johann Heinrich Miller. (*German-American Annals.* Vol. 14, p. 118 ff.)
Diffenderffer, F. R. Early German Printers of Lancaster County and the Issues of their Presses. (In Vol. VIII of the *Proceedings and Reports of the Lancaster County Historical Society.*)
—— Oldest Daily Newspaper in Lancaster. (In *Proceedings of Lancaster County Historical Society,* 1896.)
—— Newspapers of Lancaster County. (In Vol. VI of *Proceedings of Lancaster County Historical Society.*)
—— An Early Newspaper. (In Vol. XI of the *Proceedings of Lancaster County Historical Society.*)
Hildeburn, C. R. A Century of Printing. The Issues of the Press of Pennsylvania. 1685–1784. 2 vols. Philadelphia, 1885.
Ingram, J. V. Check List of American Eighteenth Century Newspapers in the Library of Congress. Washington, 1912.

Keyser, N. H. and others. History of Old Germantown. Philadelphia, 1907. (P. 427 ff. "Sower's Newspapers.")

McCulloch, William. Additional Memoranda for the History of Printing by Isaiah Thomas, Communicated by William McCulloch, 1814. (Unpublished MS. in the American Antiquarian Society, Worcester, Mass.)

Miller, Daniel. Early German American Newspapers. Lancaster, 1911. (Reprinted from Vol. XIX of the Publications of the Pennsylvania German Society.)

—— The German Newspapers of Berks County. (In the *Transactions of the Historical Society of Berks County*, Vol. III, p. 4 ff.)

North, S. N. D. History and Present Condition of the Newspapers and Periodical Press of the United States. (Part of Vol. VIII of the Census of 1880.)

Schlözer, A. L. Briefwechsel, meist statistischen Inhalts, gesammlet und zum Versuch herausgegeben. Göttingen, 1775–1781. 10 vols. (Contains a reprint of the Saur Tory paper of 1778.)

Seidensticker, Oswald. Die deutsch-amerikanische Zeitungspresse während des vorigen Jahrhunderts. (In the *Deutsch-Amerikanisches Magazin*.)

—— The First Century of German Printing in America (1728–1830). Philadelphia, 1893.

Smith, H. W. Life and Correspondence of the Reverend William Smith, D.D. Philadelphia, 1879. (Contains much interesting information about the older Saur.)

Thomas, Isaiah. The History of Printing in America. 2 vols. Second edition. 1874.

Chapter II.

Brumbaugh, M. G. A History of the German Baptist Brethren in Europe and America. Mount Morris, Illinois, 1899.

Chronicon Ephratense. A History of the Community of Seventh day Baptists at Ephrata, Lancaster, Co., Pa. Translated by J. Max Hark, D.D., Lancaster, Pa. 1889.

Dubbs, J. H. A History of the Reformed Church, German in the United States. New York, 1895.

Hallesche Nachrichten von den Vereinigten Deutschen Evangelisch-Lutherischen Gemeinen in Nord Amerika, absonderlich in Pennsylvania. (Reprinted, Vol. I, Allentown, 1886; Vol. II, Philadelphia, 1895.)

Hamilton, J. T. A History of the Moravian Church in the United States. New York, 1895.

Harbaugh, Henry. The Life of Rev. Michael Schlatter. Philadelphia, 1857.

Hinke, W. J. Life and Letters of the Reverend John Philip Boehm, Philadelphia, 1916.

Jacobs, H. E. A Short History of the Evangelical Lutheran Church in the United States. New York, 1893.
Levering, J. M. History of Bethlehem, Pennsylvania, 1741–1892. Bethlehem, 1903.
Mann, W. J. Life and Times of Henry Melchior Mühlenberg. 2 ed. Philadelphia, 1888.
Reichel, L. T. The Early History of the Church of the United Brethren (Unitas Fratrum) commonly called Moravians, in North America. Nazareth, Pa. 1888.
Sachse, J. F. The German Sectarians of Pennsylvania. 1708–1800. 2 vols. Philadelphia, 1899–1900.

Chapter III.

(Same bibliography as Chapter II.)

Seidensticker, Oswald, Geschichte der Deutschen Gesellschaft von Pennsylvanien, 1764–1876. (Republished, Philadelphia, 1917, with a second part by Max Henrici, the history of the society from 1876 to 1917.)

Chapter IV.

(Many articles in the various magazines and publications mentioned under "General Works.")

Brumbaugh, M. G. Life and Works of Christopher Dock. Philadelphia, 1908.
Dubbs, J. H. History of Franklin and Marshall College. Lancaster, 1903.
Viereck, Louis. German Instruction in American Schools. Report of Commissioner of Education, 1901, vol. I, pp. 531–708.
Weber, S. E. The Charity School Movement in Colonial Pennsylvania. (Doctor's Dissertation, University of Pennsylvania, 1905.)

Chapter V.

Haldeman, S. S. Pennsylvania Dutch: A Dialect of South German with an Infusion of English. Philadelphia, 1872.
Learned, M. D. The Pennsylvania German Dialect. Baltimore, 1889.

Chapter VI.

Mittelberger, Gottlieb. Reise nach Pennsylvanien im Jahr 1750, und Rückreise nach Teutschland im Jahr 1754. Frankfurt und Leipzig, 1756. (Translated by C. T. Eben and published in Philadelphia, 1898.)

Schöpf, Johann David. Reise durch einige der mittlern und südlichen vereinigten nordamerikanischen Staaten unternommen in den Jahren 1783 und 1784. Erlangen, 1788. (Translated and edited by Alfred I. Morrison. Published by William J. Campbell, Philadelphia, 1911.)

(These two works give a particularly unfavorable account of the Germans. For a brighter picture, see Rush's "An account of the manners of the German inhabitants of Pennsylvania," mentioned under "General Works.")

Chapters VII and VIII.

(Almost all of the publications enumerated under "General Works" contain something concerning the vocations and the political ideals of the Pennsylvania Germans.)

Davis, W. W. H. The Fries Rebellion, 1798–99; an armed resistance to the House tax law passed by Congress, July 9, 1798, in Bucks and Northampton Counties, Pennsylvania. Doylestown, Pa., 1899.

Index

Adams, 163, 165
Allen, 204
Andrä, Reverend, 42, 44
Albrecht, Johann, 24, 25, 27, 188
Anthon, 9
Armbrüster, Anthon, 99, 176, 177, 202, 203
Armbrüster, Gotthart, 8, 9, 174, 175, 176
Arndt, Jacob, 150
August, Friedrich, 46
August, Peter, 46
Bailey, Francis, 16, 180
Bärtgis, Matthias, 34, 187, 192
Barth, Joseph, 133
Barton, 27, 189, 190
Bartsch, 154
Bausman, Lottie, ix
Becker, Carl, x
Beissel, Conrad, 40
Bell, Robert, 98, 99
Billmeyer, 186, 187
Billmeyer, Andrew, 32, 201
Billmeyer, Michael, 20, 21, 22, 32, 186
Boden, 99
Boehm, Johann, 45
Böhm, Johann, 8, 88, 175
Bothe, Eastoner, 209
Braddock, 149
Brigham, Clarence S., ix, 169, 203
Brückmann, Johann, 28, 190
Brumbaugh, 169

Campbell, William J., 179, 207
Carter, 194, 196, 201
Cist, 181, 203
Cist, Carl, 24
Cist, Charles, 16, 17
Cobbett, William, 25, 97, 161
Conrad, Nicolaus, 150
Crellius, Joseph, 174
Dulheuer, Henry, 34, 187
Dunlap, John, 16, 101, 181
Eckhart, Adam, 131
Egle, William H., 33, 199
Enderlein, Michael, 77
Endresz, 19
Fahnestock, C., 199, 204
Falckener, 53
Faust, vii, 212
Forbes, General, 40
Franklin, Benjamin, 2, 3, 5, 8, 9, 171, 175, 176, 202
Fries, John, 163, 164, 165, 166
Fyring, Philip, 136
Gartley, 90
Gellert, 88, 99, 100
George, Seneca, 151
Gerrisch, George, 29, 30, 195
Geszner, 99, 100
Gettman, 165
Geyer, Andreas, 99
Geyer, John, 20, 183
Girard, Stephen, 68
Glossbrenner, 194, 196, 201
Goethe, 99, 100
Görring, Reverend, 32, 47, 79, 201

Gruber, Johann, 194
Gruber, M.A., x, 28, 190
Hagedorn, 99
Hainey, 165
Halle, 100
Hamilton, William, 26, 197, 198
Händel, William, 47, 92, 115
Handschuh, 44
Handschuh, John F., 9
Harris, Robert, 30
Hays, I.M., ix
Helmboldt, George Jr., 20, 183, 201, 202
Helmuth, 18, 49, 90, 164
Helmuth, J.C., 46
Hermann, Friedrich, 94
Herschel, 115
Hertzog, Lina, ix
Heterich, 137
Hetrich, George, 206
Hiester, Joseph, 138
Hinke, William J., x, 185, 196, 210
Holland, S., 8, 9
Hölty, 100
Hostetter, A.K., x
Hubner, 98
Hutchins, Joseph, 92
Hütter, Christian Jacob, 26, 27, 100, 101, 200
Ingram, 178, 185
Jefferson, 55
Johnson, 27, 146, 189
Josephus, Flavius, 98
Jungmann, Gottlob, 27, 28, 29, 30
Jungmann, 97, 189, 190

Kämmerer, Henrich, 19, 97, 183, 197
Kämmerer, Friedrich, 19
Kämmerer, Joseph, 19, 183, 197, 201
Kammerhof, 53
Keidel, George C., x
Keppele, Heinrich, 138
Keppele, 64
Kleist, Ewald von, 99, 100
Klopstock, 99, 100
Knauss, Ludwig, viii
Kolb, Martin, 45
Koplin, Matthias, 66, 67
Kraus, Andreas, 55
Krauth, 208
Kugler, Polly, 22
Kühmle, Johann, 68, 139
Kuhn, vii, 65, 212
Kunze, 18, 90
Kunze, J.C., 46
Lahn, Jacob, 24, 98, 100, 101, 188
Lehman, Daniel, 90
Leibert, Peter, 20, 21, 22, 186
Leitzel, Johann Wolfgang, 77
Lepper, W.D., 32, 196
Lessing, 100
Logan, 32, 79
Löser, Jacob, 81
Ludwig, 154
Luther, 87, 88
Martin, Helen Reimensnyder, viii
Mayer, B., 199, 204
Mäyer, Solomon, 31, 204
McCorde, 204

McCulloch, William, 17, 20
McKean, Governor, 31
Meiszner, 100
Melsheimer, Friedrich Valentin, 47, 92, 93
Merckel, Heinrich, 124
Meusel, 100
Michaelis, 100
Mifflin, Walter, 70
Miller, Daniel, viii
Miller, Heinrich, 7, 9, 10, 11, 12, 13, 14, 54, 55, 57, 89, 97, 142, 177, 178
Miller, Peter, 98
Miller, viii, 26, 45, 63, 98, 145, 151, 152, 153, 154, 155, 169, 177, 202, 203, 204, 211
Moliere, 100
Montgomery, Thomas Lynch, ix
Mühlenberg, F.A., 48, 116, 138
Mühlenberg, Heinrich Melchior, 5, 46, 52, 92, 109, 116, 158, 159
Müller, Anton, 150
Müller, H., 8, 9
Myers, Albert Cook, ix, x
Nyberg, 52
Ohrendorff, Reverend, 42
Pennypacker, S.W., 69, 206
Plank, 100
Plitt, 204
Pope, Paul R., x
Prowell, George R., 194
Pulasky, 155
Rabener, 99, 100
Ramler, 100
Ray, J.M., 94

Reiche, C.C., 18, 19, 35, 70, 147, 191
Reidenbach, William, 92
Reinholdt, G.C., 98
Rittenhouse, 137
Robertson, James, 13
Rothenbühler, Friedrich, 45
Sachse, 40, 169
Saint Claire, General, 159
Saur, vii, viii, 1, 12, 16, 37, 38, 39, 42, 43, 44, 57, 59, 61, 62 , 63, 66, 67, 69, 70, 73, 75, 76, 87, 88, 89, 96, 101, 106, 123, 124, 125, 134, 135, 141, 144, 146, 147, 148, 149, 151, 156, 157, 169, 171, 179, 211
Saur, Christoph, 3, 4, 5, 6, 7, 24, 61, 173, 174
Saur, Christoph Jr., 4, 13, 180
Saur, Peter, 4, 6, 7, 173, 174
Saur, Samuel, 7, 22, 34, 126, 168, 191, 193
Scheible, Johann, 137
Schiller, 126
Schlatter, Reverend, 43, 44, 47, 75, 109
Schlosser, George, 136, 154
Schneider, Jacob, 27, 28, 29, 30, 195, 199
Schnorr, Caspar, 42
Schöpf, 108, 121
Schweitzer, 19, 22, 196, 197
Seidensticker, vii, viii, 22, 26, 32, 33, 40, 169, 177, 192, 193, 195, 199
Shaaber, Andrew, ix
Shakespeare, 99
Snowden, 204
Spofford, Ernest, ix
Steiner, Melchior, 16, 17, 18, 19, 21, 113, 181, 203
Steiner, Reverend, 43, 92, 97
Stellingius, 196

Stellinius, 196
Stettinius, E., 196
Stiegel, Henrich Wilhelm, 70, 134
Stiemer, Anthon, 24, 188
Stuber, Heinrich, 90
Tanneberg, David, 46, 136
Teerstegen, 97
Thuun, 99
Thomas, Isaiah, 154, 175, 176, 202
Thwaites, R.G., 32
Timothee, Louis, 2, 3
Unger, Charles W., 191, 209
Van Bebber, Hendrick, 3
Wartemann, Reverend, 42
Weaver, Ethan Allen, x, 192
Welschantz, Jacob, 137
Weidner, Georg Adam, 70
Weiser, Conrad, 42, 150, 151
Weiss, 177, 202, 203
Weygandt, Jacob, 33, 192
Wieland, 100
Wiegand, Wilhelm, 76
Wilcocks, Henry, 31
Witzler, Reverend Jonas, 42
Wortmann, Conrad, 198
Wyeth, 204
Zindendorf, Nicholas von, 51
Zubly, Reverend, 45

Heritage Books by Don Heinrich Tolzmann:

Amana: William Rufus Perkins' and Barthinius L. Wick's History of the Amana Society, or Community of True Inspiration

Americana Germanica: Paul Ben Baginsky's Bibliography of German Works Relating to America, 1493–1800

Biography of Baron Von Steuben, the Army of the American Revolution and Its Organizer: Rudolf Cronau's Biography of Baron von Steuben

CD: German-American Biographical Index (Midwest Families)

CD: Germans, Volume 2

CD: The German Colonial Era (four volumes)

Cincinnati's German Heritage

Covington's German Heritage

Custer: Frederick Whittaker's Complete Life of General George A. Custer, Major General of Volunteers, Brevet Major General U.S. Army and Lieutenant-Colonel Seventh U.S. Cavalry

Dayton's German Heritage: Karl Karstaedt's Golden Jubilee History of the German Pioneer Society of Dayton, Ohio

Early German-American Newspapers: Daniel Miller's History

German Achievements in America: Rudolf Cronau's Survey History

German Americans in the Revolution

German Immigration to America: The First Wave

German Pioneer Life and Domestic Customs

German Pioneer Lifestyle

German Pioneers in Early California: Erwin G. Gudde's History

German-American Achievements: 400 Years of Contributions to America

German-Americana: A Bibliography

Germany and America, 1450–1700

Kentucky's German Pioneers: H. A. Rattermann's History

Lives and Exploits of the Daring Frank and Jesse James: Thaddeus Thorndike's Graphic and Realistic Description of Their Many Deeds of Unparalleled Daring in the Robbing of Banks and Railroad Trains

Louisiana's German Heritage: Louis Voss' Introductory History

Maryland's German Heritage: Daniel Wunderlich Nead's History

Memories of the Battle of New Ulm: Personal Accounts of the Sioux Uprising. L. A. Fritsche's History of Brown County, Minnesota (1916)

Michigan's German Heritage: John Andrew Russell's History of the German Influence in the Making of Michigan

Ohio's German Heritage

Outbreak and Massacre by the Dakota Indians in Minnesota in 1862: Marion P. Satterlee's Minute Account of the Outbreak, with Exact Locations, Names of All Victims, Prisoners at Camp Release, Refugees at Fort Ridgely, etc. Complete List of Indians Killed in Battle and Those Hung, and Those Pardoned at Rock Island, Iowa

The German-American Soldier in the Wars of the U.S.: J. G. Rosengarten's History

The German Element in Virginia: Herrmann Schuricht's History

The German Immigrant in America

The Pennsylvania Germans: James Owen Knauss, Jr.'s Social History

The Pennsylvania Germans: Jesse Leonard Rosenberger's Sketch of Their History and Life

www.ingramcontent.com/pod-product-compliance
Lightning Source LLC
Chambersburg PA
CBHW070733160426
43192CB00009B/1426